Gay by God

Also by Rev. Piazza

Queeries:
Questions Lesbians and Gays Have for God, second edition

The Real antiChrist:
How America Sold Its Soul

Prophetic Renewal:
Hope for the Liberal Church

Gay by God

How to be Lesbian or Gay and Christian

Rev. Michael S. Piazza

Sources of Hope Publishing
Dallas, Texas 75235

GAY BY GOD: *How to be lesbian or gay and Christian.*
Published by Sources of Hope Publishing
P.O. Box 35466
5910 Cedar Springs Road
Dallas, TX 75235
800-501-4673

Originally published as *Holy Homosexuals* 1994, 1995, 1997

ISBN 978-1-887129-10-7

Unless otherwise noted, scripture citations are taken from the New Revised Standard Version of the Bible, copyright 1989, by the Division of Christian Education of the National Council of Churches of Christ in the United States of America. Used by permission. All rights reserved.

Printed in the United States

Cover design by David Montejano
Back cover photo by Shawn Northcutt

To my family,
whose unconditional love
made me believe that was how God loves.

Table of Contents

So God created humankind in God's image,
in the image of God they were created,
male and female God created them.
Genesis 1:27

Acknowledgments

This work is possible because an incredible congregation has made a genuine commitment to developing resources for lesbian and gay people and their family and friends. The Cathedral of Hope is uncompromisingly devoted to reaching out to every person who has been excluded by their churches of origin. It has accepted nothing less than the challenge of developing a global outreach targeting lesbian and gay teenagers and gay people living in isolated or rural areas of the United States and beyond.

Almost everything about this church is miraculous. The membership, attendance and budget have more than quintupled since 1987. The Cathedral is currently in the top one percent of all churches in America in size and ministry. It is a thriving liberal and inclusive church in the heart of fundamentalism.

Our dream is to create support groups, called Circles of Hope, in communities that are not large enough to support their own including church. If you might be interested in such a group in your community, please contact the Cathedral of Hope in Dallas, Texas, USA.

In addition, our goal is to create a voice to offset the damage done by the right-wing televangelists who are using homophobia to raise funds. Our worship services are available on videotape, DVD, CD and cassette. They can also be viewed on numerous cable access stations across the country. If you would like to assist us with this program, it is likely that you can get our Sunday services aired in your community free of charge. This is a courageous church that has undertaken almost every challenge put to it. Your help could make a world of difference in bringing the good news to people in rural or isolated areas.

I also want to say a word about the Board and Staff of the Cathedral. I could never adequately thank them for their support and encouragement. In particular, I want to thank David Plunkett for the use of his editing skills. He has been a gift from God. Without David this book would not have been possible. He has read, reread, edited and re-edited this manuscript repeatedly. Thank you!

I must pay my ultimate tribute to my partner and spouse, Bill Eure. Since 1980, he has been the source of my greatest support and encouragement. Bill has had to endure numerous evenings looking at the backside of my computer. He is the most incredible gift God could have ever given me. His love has been more than I could ever have asked for.

Our lives have two additional blessings named Jerica and Jordan. Jerica was three months old when she came to our family; eight months later Jordan was born. What beautiful daughters; what bundles of pure joy and delight. I hope that, someday, this book will help them understand that homophobia is evil, not their parents' sexuality.

Finally, my greatest thanks go to God, whose love never gave up on me, even when I gave up on myself. I hope you know that the fact that you are reading a book such as this is a clear sign that God has never given up on you either.

Introduction

Perhaps her question was the result of having two gay parents, or maybe it was just that she was 13 years old. In either case, several years ago, when Texas was considering a constitutional amendment that would deny lesbian and gay taxpaying couples the same civil rights as heterosexual couples, my eldest daughter had a teacher who thought she needed to comment on the subject. This teacher, who attended a fundamentalist church, suggested that her students should encourage their parents to vote in favor of the proposed discriminatory amendment. Her rationale was rooted in something her pastor obviously had said: "God created Adam and Eve, not Adam and Steve." It was at this point that my daughter raised her hand and asked, "Excuse me, but, if that is true, then who created Adam and Steve?"

It is the contention of this book that, since every lesbian or gay person I know would tell you they were born gay, it is something God did. Proverbs 17:31 says, "The one who oppresses the poor shows contempt for his/her maker, but whoever is kind to the needy honors God." I have always thought you could substitute homosexual for the word poor: "The one who oppresses the homosexual shows contempt for his/her maker ... ." If our starting point is that every human is created in the image and likeness of God, then we ought to take great care in how we treat any of God's precious children. As a gay man, created in the image of God, I also have a responsibility to live up to my heritage by becoming as happy, healthy and holy as I can be. The hope of this book is to help all who read it cleanse their minds of the preaching and teachings that were based on a faulty assumption, and to take as our starting point that lesbian and gay people are created in the image and likeness of God. After all, if God didn't create "Adam and Steve," who did?

I know it is tough to create a new starting place for what we believe, because it was a struggle for me as well. In 1979 I was just beginning to deal honestly with the fact that, although I was an ordained United Methodist minister, I was also a homosexual man. Almost by accident, I picked up a book by Tim LaHaye entitled *The Unhappy Gays*. The book described the pathetic and wretched condition under which he believed homosexuals lived their lives. The book, without any scientific documentation, made such outlandish claims as "half the suicides in America are due to homosexuality" and "moral fidelity among homosexuals is almost unknown." LaHaye even stated categorically that, "A Christian cannot be a committed homosexual."

When I read this book in the late 1970s, I had never had a sexual relationship with another man. At that time, I did not identify yet as gay and did not understand fully what that meant. It was only the beginning of my resolve to be honest, but I recognized that, ever since I was a young child, I had always been curious about, and later attracted to, my own gender. When I was six, two cousins, who were about my age, convinced me to "play doctor." I had no interest at all in my female cousin but was very intrigued with my male cousin. There was nothing sexual about that experience, but, when sexual feelings did begin to awaken in me, I became very aware that I felt differently than society told me I would and should. Because I felt called to pastoral ministry when I was in high school, I was very motivated to keep those feelings repressed and hidden, even from myself. Then, just as I was about to confront the truth about my sexual orientation, I picked up Tim LaHaye's poisonous book. It convinced me that I had no interest in identifying myself with what he described as "the unhappy gays."

Now, many years later, I know that LaHaye was seriously mistaken and that much of what he wrote was ludicrously misinformed and twisted. What he represented about lesbian and gay people bears little, if any, resemblance to the thousands of women and men in the community with whom I minister today. Whether misrepresentations like his are deliberate or a series of misunderstandings is something only LaHaye's conscience can say for sure. Although I cannot evaluate the intention of writers and preachers like LaHaye (Jerry Falwell, James Kennedy, Phyllis Schlafly, Pat Robertson and others), I can bear personal testimony to the damage that this kind of misinformation has done in my life and in the lives of thousands of others. These radical-right fundamentalists have wounded, and in many cases destroyed, the happiness, health and holiness of thousands of innocent people—people whose only "fault" was to have been born with an attraction to people of their own gender.

In my case, his book, and others like it, kept me ensnared in a lifestyle that was dishonest and filled with painful conflicts. It did not change who I was, but it did keep me living a lie and feeling great guilt over something I had not done. I prayed, fasted, worked three jobs to pay for therapy, attended Oral Roberts University, went to faith healers and deliverers, and tried everything I could think of to persuade God to change my sexual orientation. None of it worked, and each time I was left feeling more depressed and hopeless. By that time, I had been a devoted Christian for almost 20 years and a minister of the Gospel for eight years, but a day came when I wondered if God might not have utterly abandoned me. If LaHaye and his ilk were right and I could not be gay and Christian, and if I could not persuade God to make me not gay, then my only option was not to be a Christian. That was the one thing in my life that I had never considered optional.

Fortunately for me, God had other ideas. Through a seminary classmate named Paul Tucker, I found a congregation that was gay affirming, something I never even knew existed. Paul was the first openly gay man I had ever met. He, too, had been a United Methodist and felt called to the ministry. Paul had pastored a small church while in college but had come to recognize that, as a gay man, the Methodist church was not the place for him. That day, as he told me his story, I became increasingly aware that he was also telling my story. The liberation my soul felt at that moment was so great that it felt remarkably like being born again, again. What a miracle to discover that not only did God know all about my sexuality, but that it did not affect God's love for me one bit. That day, Paul's witness and the existence of a community of lesbian and gay Christians brought incredible healing and optimism when I was near the end of my hope.

During the more than 30 years that I have been a pastor, I have counseled hundreds of people who had given up all hope of living happy, healthy and holy lives because of the lies some homophobic pastor, priest, parent or teacher told them. For those of us who grew up in evangelical or conservative Christian homes, wrestling with faith and sexuality is difficult enough. For many lesbian and gay people, the struggle for too long resulted in only two options: sacrificing one's sexual integrity or giving up one's faith. Hundreds, perhaps thousands, of men and women, young and old, have told me of their tortured journeys as they tried to give up being gay but could not. They believed their only option was to give up being Christian. One young man said, in all honesty, "Hey, if I am going to hell anyway, I may as well enjoy the trip." I never could convince him that he had an alternative. That young man is dead now, the victim of a drug overdose.

The homo-hatred of the Religious Right has driven so many beautifully gifted women and men into the arms of suicide, alcoholism, promiscuity and self-destruction. It is impossible to overstate the damage done in human lives when people are made to believe they cannot be children of the God who created them. I reread LaHaye's book after finding a copy in a used bookstore. The copy obviously had belonged originally to a parent who had discovered that their son or daughter was gay. The notes scribbled in the margin of the book were often pleas to God. My heart breaks for that dear soul, tormented by LaHaye's suggestion that perhaps they were somehow to blame for the utterly hopeless picture he painted for that parent's child. As a father myself, I can only imagine the sheer agony that parent must have felt. The fact that society's ignorance, fear and prejudice allow these right-winged homophobes to poison so many innocent lives without rebuke from the Church of Jesus Christ is outrageous to me. Their faces should be on wanted posters in post offices because their poison has resulted in mass murder.

It is little wonder that so many homosexuals view the Judeo-Christian faith as an enemy that is out to destroy them. That has certainly been the case for the most visible representatives of the faith: media ministers. The silence of better informed Christians and Jews who disagree with the Religious Right has been deafening. Those lesbian and gay people who have succeeded in retaining their faith have done so either through extraordinary effort or by the blessed intervention of institutions such as the Cathedral of Hope, the United Church of Christ, and the Universal Fellowship of Metropolitan Community Churches.

My purpose for writing this book is to provide a resource for those who are still struggling to reconcile their faith and sexual orientation. My goal is to spare others the anguish that some of us suffered while struggling to keep our faith or to regain it. If just one mother or father reads this book and is better able to accept her or his daughter or son, then this effort has been of value. Faith should not be a barrier between parents and their children.

It is also my hope that those of us who have discovered that being lesbian or gay is a gift from God might benefit from a fuller understanding of that reality. There are still thousands of people to whom we need to bring the good news that they do not need to relinquish either their sexuality or their faith. In good evangelical fashion, we must witness to them the reality that you can be gay or lesbian and Christian. Perhaps this book will help you answer some of their questions. You are now an ambassador of this good news.

There are wonderful alternatives to the "unhappy gay" described by people like LaHaye, Robertson and Falwell. There are thousands of lesbian and gay people who have discovered how to become the happy, healthy and holy people God created them to be. My prayer is that you will not settle for anything less in your life!

At the Cathedral of Hope, I've learned to be quiet and listen for the Lord. To wait on Him. As I look back on my life, I know I have missed the voice of the Lord. I was expecting a wind or an earthquake, not a still small voice. What overwhelms me is that He has always been there with me; I've just missed hearing Him.

Peter Soper
Dallas, TX

Chapter 1
Coming out at 30,000 Feet

You shall know the truth, and the truth shall set you free.

Jesus

Scott was the most active member of our Methodist Youth Fellowship. A gentle, soft-spoken young man, he seemed to have a profound hunger for God and a great love for the Church. It always amazed me to look out at the Sunday night congregation and see his bright smile in a sea of white hair. He often would stop by my office with some excuse for chatting. He was very bright and serious, and I always enjoyed our conversations. But there was something about him that was troubled and troubling. I kept encouraging him to talk to our youth director, a college student much closer to his age.

Every time Scott and I talked, I wanted to ask him if something else was on his mind. He seemed to struggle with guilt and shame, though I could never figure out what could so distress a healthy young man. One day his eyes brightened as he talked about a fellow student who had become a new friend. It was not until we had talked for several minutes that I recognized that the boy he spoke about so enthusiastically might have been more than just a friend. He said nothing sexual in nature, but Scott clearly was enamored of this young man. He grew increasingly quiet as he described what he felt. He was confused, frightened and ashamed, not about any acts, but simply because of the affection he felt. Scott was terrified the boy might reject him, and I suspect he also was afraid I might reject him. The conversation made me very uncomfortable. I tried to reassure him that I did not judge him, but it's very possible he interpreted my discomfort as condemnation.

The reality was that Scott's story was hitting too close to home.

He failed to come by the office for a week or two. I confess that my own inner turbulence so absorbed me that I hardly noticed his absence. This young man's turmoil and his honesty about his feelings had made me feel very ashamed of how I was handling my own feelings of attraction toward men. But I rationalized that, if I wanted to continue serving as a United Methodist minister, I had to suppress those feelings, or at least keep them secret. That's why I restrained myself from sharing my own struggle with Scott.

No one will ever really know what happened one afternoon when Scott went to his father's office to talk to him. What is known, however, is that Scott left the office, made his way to the roof of a building in midtown Atlanta, and jumped to his death.

I was still at the office when they called with the news. I am sure my colleagues were as stunned as I was, but my reaction was so strong that I had to return to my office and lock the door. Rarely has my body been so racked with grief and guilt. On that day I promised God never again to hesitate to tell the truth about myself. Could I have saved Scott? No one can say for certain. What I can say for sure is that I am determined never to struggle with such questions again. Ironically, the young man who was our youth director in that Methodist church also committed suicide several years later. His death also was related to his sexuality and spirituality.

Suicides and attempted suicides by lesbian and gay teenagers are epidemic. By many estimates, they are four times that of heterosexual teens. To me, it is no wonder. These young people often grow up in Christian homes where their parents or pastors tell them that "God so loved the world ... ." On the other hand, these kids also learn, early on, that there are exceptions—that somehow God's love is not strong enough to include them if they are too different. Their "sin," something out of their control, is portrayed as horrible, ugly and disgusting. They often struggle to change, hide and pretend, but, in the end, the feelings remain. While they are taught that God cannot love them unless they change, it seems that God will not change them, so they are left without hope.

Over the years, many people have claimed that God has transformed their sexual orientation. They say God removed or healed their homosexuality. But of the hundreds of people I personally know who went through such changes, **every one** of them eventually came to realize that the only thing removed by all those "transformations" was their integrity.

Out of the more than 3,000 people who attend our church, several hundred of them were once "ex-gays." What makes their stories even more tragic is that, under their religious delusion of being "delivered," they often married and, in many cases, had children. Their spouses and children often became additional victims of the Religious Right, which forces so many women and men to live lies in order to try to save their mortal souls.

This torment of innocent young people must stop. Homophobic preachers are killing these teenagers just as surely as if they had slipped the noose over their necks or pushed them from the roof. This is no longer a matter of sincere people disagreeing. It is abuse, persecution and accessory to suicide.

Sandi was reared in a nominally Jewish home, but, as a teenager, she went with a friend to a revival meeting at the local Assembly of God. When, at the end of the service, the preacher invited the congregation to step forward and accept Christ, Sandi responded to the call. It was an emotional experience, one that left her feeling like a different person.

While some discount these kinds of experiences, I know many people who were genuinely born again at an altar.

The "good news" of her conversion did not exactly thrill Sandi's Jewish parents, but, to their credit, they accepted Sandi's choice and supported her new-found faith. Secretly, they assumed that this was a phase that she would soon outgrow. It was not a phase, and, as the years went by, Sandi became increasingly active in her church.

Then, at the age of 18, disaster struck. Sandi fell in love with a young woman named Wendy whom she had met in her Sunday School class. To make matters worse, Wendy was the pastor's daughter. The young women were unclear about what was going on in their lives. They did not have a context in which to put their feelings. Although nothing sexual had taken place, they seemed to sense that, if people ever found out about their relationship, they would not be warmly supported.

It was at another revival that they learned, to their horror, what their feelings were called. The visiting preacher talked about the terrible things God did to the city of Sodom because of "homosexuality." He described, in great detail, the loathing that he believed God felt for people who participated in such "deviant" lifestyles. What this preacher lacked in education and intellect, he made up in fervor and passion. At the end of the message, he gave an invitation for those who might be possessed by the "demon of homosexuality" to come forward and be delivered from the devil.

Without really thinking about the consequences, Sandi answered the invitation, just as she had done several years earlier. Both the visiting preacher and her pastor anointed her with oil and spent nearly half an hour casting out the "demon" from her. When they were done, they pronounced her delivered, and the entire church praised God for a miracle. Sandi could not tell that she felt any better, but she sensed that something had definitely happened.

The next day, as usual, when she got to school, she went to meet Wendy, but her friend was nowhere to be found. It was not until her third period algebra class that she heard that Wendy's parents had taken her out of school and were going to send her to a private religious school in another town. Sandi could not believe that was true, and she rushed home after classes to call her friend to get the real story.

Wendy's mom answered the phone and explained that Wendy could not talk to her. In fact, she said, it probably would be best if Sandi simply did not call anymore. Before the week was out, the whole school had heard about Sandi's "sin," and she was utterly ostracized and ridiculed. As painful as that was, the greater pain was losing Wendy. Sandi had never felt so alone in her life. The pain told her that the preacher had been right. Homosexual love was hell, but not the kind he meant.

Eventually, Sandi got married. I met her when she came to my office for counseling after her second child was born. She was in a deep depression and was afraid of what she might do to herself or her child. She had decided to divorce her husband because she was ruining his life and her own. Although she respected and liked the man she married, there was no passion or real love. Clearly, the whole thing had been a charade. Sandi was a good mother, and she continued to share custody of the children. But she felt that, since the day of the revival, her life had been a mess. She counted that as the last truly honest and happy day of her life.

Her question for me that day was, "Why?" Why was it that the deliverance "didn't take?" Why were the love and happiness she knew with Wendy never repeated in her life? Why did the Church hate homosexuals so much that it would rather see them suffer alone than be happy with someone of the same gender? Sandi had been the victim of an undoubtedly well-meaning preacher who had damaged her life and created a painful situation for others.

In February 1981 the conservative evangelical publication "Christianity Today" reported as fraudulent the claims made by a number of ministries about "ex-gays." There have been many nonreligious studies since then that support their findings. The false hope of transformation has left too many people only feeling more despair. While it is true that sufficiently motivated people probably can suppress their natural orientations, why should they have to suffer a lifetime of deception in the name of the God of Truth?

At the Cathedral of Hope, we minister to hundreds of people who have been victims of these ministries and who have discovered that all those programs really offered were lifetimes of denial, repression and loneliness. Falsehood can never be the foundation of a happy, healthy, holy life. The late Rev. Sylvia Pennington, a heterosexual woman who spent her life ministering to lesbians and gays, summarized this reality in a book entitled *Ex-gays? There Are None!*

Hearing television preachers declare, so conclusively, that God can change homosexuals into heterosexuals infuriates me. I wonder how many innocent teenagers they have condemned to years of torturous struggle and self-deception with those words. I have never talked to an "ex-gay" who, when they were honest, would not admit that all they were doing was repressing their natural affections. That is fine for them if they wish to live that way, but there should be no claims that these persons have had their sexual orientation changed.

Michael Bussee and Gary Cooper were ex-gay evangelists and two of the founders of Exodus International, an organization for those who have been "converted" from homosexuality by an experience with Jesus Christ. In 1979,

Bussee and Cooper finally found the courage to admit that their own method had never really changed them and that they were in love with one another. Both men publicly admitted that the program was a lie and subsequently tried to undo the damage they did through Exodus. Tragically, the crusade continues, though hundreds of people like Bussee are now telling the truth that, for them, the movement is based on a lie. It is true that people who are sufficiently motivated can be encouraged, supported or coerced into suppressing their natural orientation, at least for a time. However, I have never met a genuine "ex-gay," though I have known dozens of miserable pretenders.

For uninformed preachers to claim that Jesus can change one's sexual orientation is as ludicrous as suggesting that He can change one's race. Perhaps He can, but He won't. That is how God made you and who God intended you to be. Such easy and pat answers only reflect ignorance of the complex issues or callous disregard for the happiness of the children of God. I've never known a person who made themselves gay, and Jesus is not so arrogant as to change something God has done. Unfortunately, some of Jesus' followers are arrogant enough to try.

An estimated 6 to 10 percent of the population is homosexual; about the same percentage is left-handed. There are other similarities as well. For example, studies have documented, rather conclusively, that genetics largely determines sexuality as well as handedness. We do not choose to be right- or left-handed. No one has ever adequately explained why a 90 percent majority of all people are right-handed. Just a couple of generations ago, school teachers tried to force all children to be right-handed. Many left-handed people learned to write with their right hands and may have done so all of their lives. That does not mean that they ever became right-handed or that using the right hand ever became natural and normal. Unfortunately, many lesbian and gay people have lived most of their lives acting as though they were heterosexual. Once they can acknowledge their true orientation, it is like left-handed people at last being allowed to use the hand that is natural for them.

Utilizing religious guilt and shame to motivate homosexual people to behave heterosexually is **not** conversion! Lesbian and gay people can act as if they are heterosexuals, but that does not change their natural orientation any more than "acting" like an Asian would change their race. It simply allows homophobic people to feel more comfortable because the people around them act like them. Of much more benefit to everyone is the acknowledgment that, like left-handedness, homosexuality is simply a difference of God's creation that all should celebrate.

Celebration of diversity greatly increases the richness of the fabric of humanity. Conversely, compelling conformity through societal and religious pressure seriously diminishes the beautiful spectrum of what God has created. We treasure the variety of flowers in life's garden, but differences among members of our own species somehow threaten us. This fear of diversity is a partial explanation for the various prejudices that still irrationally plague our society.

The scriptures begin with a clear and consistent message. All that is was created by God, and all that was created was pronounced by the Creator to be "good, very good." If genetics determines a person's sexuality, it is then as accurate to say that God created a diversity of human sexuality just as surely as God created a variety of races, hair colors and body types.

Even conservative psychologists believe that the first few years of a person's life play a large part in forming their sexual orientation. Only the most grossly misinformed believe that a person consciously chooses her or his sexuality at some point prior to turning four or five. It is easy enough to see that, if a choice was possible, fewer would choose homosexuality given our culture's abuse of, and prejudice toward, lesbians and gays.

The writer of Proverbs records the following bit of wisdom in chapter 17, verse 5: "The person that mocks the poor despises their maker." As gay and lesbian adults, we must live with our sexual orientation just as we must live with our race, eye color and handedness. Although we can live a lie and pretend to be something we are not, the truth remains and we end up despising the God who created us. For people to mock, scorn or condemn us for a condition beyond our control is to mock, scorn or condemn the One who made us.

The overwhelming message of the Bible is that the two most basic features of the nature of God are justice and mercy. It is utterly impossible for God to behave in a way contrary to this nature. To punish some for something they did not do, or to judge some as sinful for being the individuals God created them to be, is neither merciful nor just. It is ironic that people who claim to take God's word seriously are able to disregard something so basic and pervasive. Having said that, we must ask ourselves if we really do believe in a God who is merciful and just. My own inconsistencies remind me, at the oddest times, how difficult it is to live out what I say I believe about God.

Many years ago, I was attending a conference in Anaheim, California. The flight back to Dallas was an unmitigated disaster. I had attended back-to-back conferences, so I was tired and ready to be home. I got to Los Angeles International Airport early and turned in my rental car, only to discover that the flight had been delayed for two hours. I had plenty of work to do, so I figured I'd make the best of it. However, engineers do not design airports for reading and writing, especially the one in Los Angeles.

So I did not get much accomplished and passed the hours mostly in frustration.

Two-and-a-half hours later, the boarding process began. The fellow behind me in line was furiously trying to fill his lungs with as many carcinogens as possible. Since I am allergic to cigarette smoke, he was not making a friend of me. My sinuses clogged instantly, but he was doing a very good job of ignoring my best Bette Davis glare.

After boarding, I looked around, surprised at how crowded the flight was after being delayed almost three hours. Finally on the plane, we sat and sat. Thirty minutes later, the captain came on the intercom to tell us that they were having trouble with something on the control panel in the cockpit, that mechanics were working on the problem, and that we should be underway soon. Those kinds of announcements are so reassuring.

Twenty minutes later, we pushed back from the gate. We then spent another 10 or 15 minutes at the end of the runway. At last, the captain told us that the plane was having some hydraulic problems, and we would have to return to the gate. We disembarked, and, about an hour later, they loaded us back on the same plane. Guess who was again standing in line behind me puffing away!

By the time I dropped into my seat, I was angry, frustrated and thoroughly exhausted. For some reason, the second attempt at this flight was even more crowded than the first. This time I had a seatmate. I looked him over, and he met my standards for the occasion. He was sober, he was clean, and he was not smoking.

I moved my briefcase so he could sit, and, while the flight attendant went through the safety instructions for the second time, I dug in my briefcase for the things I needed to get some work done. "Still got work to do, huh?" I looked at my seatmate and nodded. He seemed nice, in his early 50s and well dressed.

The plane took off over the Pacific, and, for a few minutes, the flight was quite bumpy. (Why do they have to fly so far west before they turn around to fly east?)

"Wonder if there are sharks down there." It was my seatmate again.

"Don't worry," I said sarcastically, "your seat cushion serves as a flotation device." He did not seem comforted by my pastoral care.

Soon the flight attendants were passing through the cabin with refreshments. He got a coffee. I got a Diet Coke. Then I began to struggle to open that little packet of peanuts. (Why do they seal them like they are a national treasure?)

He watched me struggle with that packet for a few moments before remarking, "You must be a preacher."

"Why do you say that? Are most preachers uncoordinated?" I asked.

"Oh, no," he said, "most people would be cursing by now, and, besides, I noticed the Bible in your briefcase."

I never really answered his question. I knew if I told him I was a preacher, he would ask what denomination. Without my answering, that is exactly what he asked. "I'm the pastor of the Cathedral of Hope Metropolitan Community Church of Dallas," I said and started writing furiously, hoping to avoid what I knew would be the next question.

"What kind of church is that?" he asked. With that, I put away my work because it was clear I was not going to get anything done. Still, I had not answered his question, which he must have thought was odd. I was not really sure what he was asking. Was he asking if we were Protestant or Catholic or Orthodox? Was he wondering if we were a fundamentalist church or a liberal church?

"Well," I said as fast as I could, "the Metropolitan Community Church is a Protestant denomination with about 300 congregations worldwide. It was founded in 1968 by Reverend Troy Perry, and the church in Dallas is the largest church in the denomination. What do you do for a living?" I did not want to know. I'd already guessed he was in sales of some kind.

"Oh, I sell water pumps," he said. "What does your church believe?"

He would not give up. When people find out that you are a preacher, they either want to talk about religion, which I think is the most boring thing in the world, or act as if they are afraid to be themselves. It is almost as if they think I will tell God on them the next time we talk.

I love to talk to people about Jesus and what He can do for them, but the last thing I want to do on a Friday night strapped in at 30,000 feet is to get into a theological debate with a conservative, middle-aged, middle-class, white male.

"Oh," I said, "our church is pretty orthodox in what we believe. We believe in God and Jesus and the Holy Spirit. We read the Bible and pray ..."

"What is it that makes you different, then?" For just a moment, I thought about using my strongest preacher's voice to tell him so everyone on the plane could hear. Then I'd bet he would have left me alone. Unfortunately, we were still an hour from Dallas, and I was not sure I wanted to spend an hour pinned against the wall by a rabid fundamentalist.

If I had not been so tired, I might have risen to the challenge, but, again, I took the easy way out. "Well," I said, "the one thing that is different about our church is that we believe in the inclusive nature of the gospel. We believe 'God so loved the world,' and we don't exclude anyone from that love."

He was quiet a moment and then said, "You ordain women, don't you?"

I thought, "Buddy, you don't know the half," but my mouth said, "Yes, in fact we do." For the next 20 minutes, we had a heated discussion about women's issues, and I figured he finally had written me off as a liberal, pinko-commie and would now leave me alone.

I read in silence for about 10 minutes, and just as I felt the plane begin its descent into the Dallas/Fort Worth airport he said to me, "What does your church believe about homosexuality?" There it was. I had worked for two hours to avoid the subject, but there it was. I'm not sure how much time really passed while I thought about all of this, but soon I confessed that our church has a primary outreach to lesbian and gay people and that I am a gay man. Well, that shut him up. He did not say anything for a while. The seatbelt sign came on as we made our final descent into DFW airport.

We were just about to touch down when American Airlines provided another surprise. Thirty feet from the ground, we suddenly pulled up sharply and took off again. For a few moments there was no explanation, and, since we had already had mechanical problems, I think even the flight attendants assumed the worst.

Shortly, the captain came on to tell us that another plane had landed in front of us and had not managed to clear the runway, so we had to go around again. There was no problem, but it would take another 20 minutes for us to get in position for another landing.

With that, the fellow turned toward me and said, "It looks like we're going to be together for another 20 minutes."

"Yeah, great," I thought. Then I noticed he had gotten very serious.

Then he asked, "Can I tell you something?"

"Sure," I said, and he began to tell me about his youngest son, Timmy, who he thought was gay. He had never really talked to him about it, but he knew it was probably true. The past week, while he was in Los Angeles, his wife had called to say that their son was in the hospital.

He had asked them to come as soon as they could. They were probably going to drive down that night after he landed.

Then he said to me, "There isn't anyone in my life I can talk to about this, but I am so scared that if my son is gay and dies of AIDS, he'll go to hell. At least that's what my preacher says. What do you think?"

I spent the next 20 minutes talking gently to this father about a God who is love and who is much kinder than some of us who claim to speak for God. I told him some facts about AIDS and how it was a virus, not divine retribution. I gave him a copy of our pamphlet on "Homosexuality and Christianity." Mostly, though, I told him that he really only needed to look into his own heart.

"You and your wife obviously love your son very much," I said. "Would you send Timmy to hell just for being gay?"

"Of course not," he replied.

"And do you think God is any less loving a parent than you are?"

He shook his head, his face brightening a bit. "Pray for us," he said, and I assured him that I would.

The wheels of the plane had screeched against the pavement, but I had not even noticed. It was only as the plane rolled to a stop and people around us began to get up that we realized the flight was over. I stood up to get off, but he said that he was going on.

As I stepped into the aisle, he took my hand, and, with tears in his eyes, said, "You know, I think God arranged this flight for me."

I've thought about that family many times and wished I had been more courageous sooner. What if that man had not been so persistent? How many others could I have helped but missed my chance by staying in that prison we call a closet? I almost made the same mistake with this guy that I made with Scott, so many years before.

Yes, I think God arranged for us to fly together that day so I could tell him about the God who made his son Timmy and who loves him very much. I also think God arranged for you and me to take this brief journey together so I could tell you the same thing.

I had always believed that to live my life with integrity, I had to be a whole person. That meant living a life that was not compartmentalized. Living a life where my sexuality, my spirituality, my politics and my integrity were reconciled. I needed a faith that could not only accept who I was on Sunday, but who I was all week long. Only as a whole person, fully integrated with all the facets of my self could I live that "abundant life" Jesus spoke about.

Through the fellowship of the diverse congregation; through the richness of the music; through the depth of the ministry, both behind the pulpit and in the congregation, I found the words of Jesus. Not just words being spoken by the ministers, but words lived out in the lives of the members of the church. These people were the body of Christ, working to follow His teachings in their own lives. That was impressive!

Hardy Haberman
Dallas, Texas

Chapter 2
Using the Bible as a Sword

*A Closer Look at Scriptures used to Attack
Lesbian and Gay People*

In 1850, two-thirds of the people in this country identified themselves as Baptist, Methodist or Presbyterian. Those three denominations shaped the moral outlook of the nation. In the South, all three did an effective job of providing ethical justification for the practice of slavery.

The Southern Baptist church exists today because Baptists in the south insisted that slavery was God's will for both whites and blacks. A Baptist clergyman from Culpepper City, Virginia named Thornton Stringfellow wrote a book entitled *Slavery Scriptural and Statistical*.

Rev. Stringfellow quoted extensively from Old Testament stories, as well as the writings of St. Paul. His strongest argument was that, in the early church, they did not argue for freeing the slaves but rather for converting them to Christianity. The Rev. Stringfellow concluded with the words:

> *The institution of slavery is full of mercy, offering
> the African heathen the message of the gospel.*

Well, I doubt the slaves saw it that way. It is no secret that, for years, the church justified the horrors of one people owning another. How tragic that an institution whose message was supposedly liberation of the oppressed and sacred human worth gave moral justification for the systematic inferiorization of an entire race. It supported the repugnant practice of slavery by taking scripture out of its historic context and reading into it its own prejudices.

In October 1632, Galileo Galilei was forced by the church, under the threat of torture, to repudiate his theory that the earth was round and rotated around the sun. Biblical fundamentalists insisted that, since the Bible speaks of the four corners of the earth, the earth must be flat.

Of course, as students of American History know, in places like Salem, Massachusetts, religious leaders used a primitive reading of scripture to justify witch trials in this country.

Less than 100 years ago, the Church used the Bible to oppose women's suffrage, and, in our own lifetime, the church in the South was largely responsible for defeating the Equal Rights Amendment. Even today, using scripture and tradition, the Roman Catholic and Orthodox churches still bar women from ordination. The Southern Baptists have taken similar stands in recent years. They seem to have entirely missed the fact that, given the sexism of his day, Jesus' ministry was actually an act of radical inclusion of women.

In the 1960s, from the pulpit of First Baptist Church, Dallas' own W. A. Criswell, the father of the modern fundamentalist movement, called racial integration a heresy. He also declared the Bible the inerrant word of God on this and all matters. Before his death Rev. Criswell admitted that he had been mistaken about racial integration, though he never confessed to his erroneous understanding of the Bible.

In agreement with Rev. Criswell in the '60s was the Rev. Jerry Falwell, who called *Brown vs. the Board of Education*, the Supreme Court's decision to end public school segregation, a "satanic plot." He also reportedly called Nelson Mandela a communist sympathizer. All across the South scripture was misused to support what we now understand to be racist views.

The Bible has so frequently been misunderstood, misinterpreted and misused that it should come as little surprise that homosexuality is just one more example of the abuse of these ancient sacred words.

I also want to note that it has only been in the last 100 years or so that fundamentalists began treating the Bible like a divinely-delivered Ouija board. For 2,000 years no one ever seriously suggested that the Bible was inerrant or infallible. Suddenly, and I believe arrogantly, fundamentalists began declaring that they are able to read the Bible and conclusively know the mind of God. Today, beyond a handful of fundamentalist seminaries, no reputable scholars would support such a view.

In reality, the average person can't read a 2,000-year-old book and interpret it without significant education and study. For example, no one is expected to read Homer's "Iliad" or "Odyssey," which are about the same age as some of the Bible, without some college-level preparation.

As a result, conservative preachers can exploit that ignorance by interpreting the Bible **for** people in a way that persuades their listeners to think and believe as the preacher does. Claiming to have the sole correct understanding of a 2,000-year-old document, which you say is infallible and is from God, gives you great power over those who can't do that for themselves. That is purely sinful arrogance.

Whenever you try to talk to people about what the Bible says, the first thing you must establish is what you and they believe the Bible is and is not. If they have been brainwashed into believing that the way their church or preacher interprets the Bible is the only correct way, or that the Bible is some antique book of science, history and social education, then conversations about what the Bible does or doesn't say are futile.

Most thinking people understand the Bible to be a 2,000-year-old document that has been translated repeatedly and interpreted differently in almost every generation. The Bible is not a single book with a single author and a single understanding. I personally own more than 30 different translations of the Bible, including one that draws on 26 different translations of the New Testament alone. The Bible is/was:

- a collection of writings by dozens of authors;
- gathered over many centuries;
- translated by hundreds of scholars;
- interpreted by thousands of theologians and preachers with a wide variety of education.

Each translator, interpreter and reader brings their own faith, experience, beliefs and prejudices. It is little wonder that we have no common language with which to discuss the Bible. Yet, fundamentalists speak of the Bible as if it were a monograph that **everyone** reads and understands the same way.

The average person is fairly illiterate about the Bible and is even more uninformed about what churches other than their own believe about it. Most people don't know that there are **many** translations and **many** understandings. They **assume** one book, one understanding.

When someone begins an argument by saying "Well, the Bible says," I stop them and say, "Which Bible? Which translation?" And if they tell me the King James Version, I love to say, "Okay, but you know King James was gay, don't you?" If that doesn't bring the conversation to a halt, I usually ask why they think there are so many different translations. If the scholars don't agree on what the Bible says, why do you think we'll agree or that we have to?

Arguing over how scriptures are understood is seldom productive. But getting people to actually think about what they believe the Bible is and isn't might help them be more open to the possibility that what they have always thought or been told could be wrong. I'd suggest avoiding, whenever possible, arguments based on the Bible. They rarely persuade anyone and generally pit ignorance against illiteracy.

As we begin to look at what the scripture does and does not say to and about lesbian and gay people, we must begin by being honest. There is great danger that we, too, may do what the fundamentalists have done. They have misused the Bible to justify their abusive and self-serving prejudice. After being attacked so often with the Bible, it is sorely tempting to use that same weapon to defend ourselves and to attack our adversaries. Although it might temporarily relieve our pain, in the long run, it would make us more like those who attack us. That is too high a price.

What follows is in no way intended to be a definitive exegesis, or analysis, of the various relevant passages of scripture on the subject. Nor is it an attempt to make an original academic contribution to the available literature. Biblical and historical scholars such as Robin Scroggs, John Boswell and Virginia Mollenkott can better do that work. What we will do is look at the passages as simply and straightforwardly as possible. The goal is to let the average lay person who grew up in an evangelical background understand that the Bible is not the enemy of lesbian and gay people. The hope is that you can gain confidence and sufficient insight to be able to help others who are still struggling with this dilemma.

Whenever we study the Bible or listen to another person's interpretation, we must always compare that revelation about God to the one that Jesus brought. Does the image of God that the teacher or preacher presents resemble the God of love that Jesus Christ revealed? Is it also fair to ask that same question when we read the Bible? If the picture of God in a passage is less merciful or just than the God of

Jesus, then it is likely that the picture is underdeveloped.

First, we will look at what are commonly called the "clobber passages." Those are the scriptures the Religious Right uses to attack lesbian and gay people. It is easy enough to see that, in the past, fundamentalists have misused the same scriptures to justify slavery. In the next section, we will look at some stories you likely never heard in Sunday School. Hopefully, these stories will help you better understand how your sexuality and spirituality fit together as gifts from the same God. Perhaps a fresh look at these scriptures will release us to sing again the words of that wise gospel hymn:

> *Beyond the sacred page I seek thee, Lord.*
> *My spirit pants for thee, O living word.*

The Hebrew Scripture

Onan

First, let me call your attention to an obscure story in Genesis 38. In those days having children was imperative to the Jews' survival. The strange story of Onan reflects the Jewish understanding of human sexuality. In the story, Onan practices birth control by withdrawing and ejaculating on the ground. Soon thereafter, Onan dies. The writer of the story blames his death on the fact that he wasted his seed, though I wonder how on earth the author knew what Onan did with his seed.

In that day, the common assumption was that the man carried the seed of human life and the woman served only as an incubator until the seed was fully developed. According to that understanding, what Onan did was kill a possible child that was desperately needed by the community. This attitude also shaped how ancient Jews viewed homosexual acts. To them, two men having sex also destroyed the desperately needed unborn children. Since women were only incubators, there are no references to lesbian acts in the Hebrew scripture.

Onan's story reflects the reality of the ancient Hebrews. Today, we know they were wrong on several counts. Science has given us a revelation that they did not have. Hence, in Western Christianity, only the Roman Catholic hierarchy retains the primitive bias against birth control, and even it no longer considers it a capital offense. The coming of Jesus revealed the naivete of some perceptions of God. Psychology has proven that ancient understandings of sexual orientation were equally outmoded. The human community no longer has a desperate need for procreation. Indeed, the fact that lesbian and gay people tend not to have children is a healthy reality for the human race. Although even the most ardent fundamentalists would not advocate the death penalty for something like what Onan did, they still use the same primitive understanding and rationale as the foundation for their condemnation of homosexuals.

Leviticus

The Bible never really talks about homosexuality, at least not in the way we understand the subject today. Our modern understanding of homosexuality only developed around 100 years ago. Biblical writers could not have dealt with psychosexual orientation any more than they could have discussed nuclear fusion or space travel. Of the 23,114 verses in the Hebrew scripture, only two refer to homosexual acts. My friend Lynn Lavner, a lesbian comedienne, notes that "the Bible contains six admonishments to homosexuals and

362 admonishments to heterosexuals. That doesn't mean that God doesn't love heterosexuals. It's just that they need more supervision."

Both Hebrew verses dealing with homosexual behavior are contained within the Holiness Code found in the book of Leviticus, the third book of the Bible. Today, even the most devout Jew no longer adheres to the full Levitical code. Generally, Christians find only a few selected passages relevant. In his book *The Act of Marriage*, fundamentalist author Tim LaHaye explained that the Levitical injunctions that prohibited a man from having sex with his wife during menstruation are no longer relevant. Changes in sanitation and scientific advances in our day have made that code obsolete, he suggests. The irony is that LaHaye draws heavily on the Levitical passages to explain his condemnation of homosexuality. He quotes a verse commanding the death penalty for a man lying with another man and follows that verse with these words: "This may seem cruel and inhuman treatment by today's standards, but our leniency has caused today's widespread problems."

More thoughtful people dismiss these passages in Leviticus as irrelevant, since we do not follow the remainder of that book's instructions. Most people eat pork and shellfish, wear clothes made from two kinds of fabric, allow women to wear red, and plant two kinds of seed in the same field. The Holiness Code prohibited all these things.

Although we may be tempted to simply dismiss these passages, it is still important that we understand them because they have provided the impetus for so many of the Church's punitive attitudes against lesbian and gay people. They are strongly worded verses that instruct us to pose the death penalty for violations:

*You shall not lie with a male as with a woman; it is
an abomination.*

Leviticus 18:22

*If a man lies with a male as with a woman, both of
them have committed an abomination; they shall be
put to death; their blood is upon them.*

Leviticus 20:13

Both verses use the word "abomination." That
word occurs six times in the book of Leviticus. Each
time, it refers to acts that might have been committed by
barbarians—pagan people who, in that day, lived around
the Jews and worshiped false gods. Judaism was one of the
few faiths that did not utilize temple prostitutes. For the
Hebrews, male homosexual acts became associated with the
idolatry of worshiping the gods of the surrounding people.

Worshiping the gods of the people around them
could lead to the destruction, or at least the assimilation, of
the Hebrews. Thus, the Levitical codes prescribed the death
penalty for male homosexual acts. The strength of that
condemnation has provided a strong foundation for much
of the homo-hatred in our society. As you will note in the
following verses, capital punishment was also the penalty
for having sex with a slave, cursing parents, committing
adultery, having sex with your stepmother or stepson, for a
man who had sex with a mother and her daughter, bestiality,
dealing with wizards, prostitution and blasphemy:

*If a man has sexual relations with a woman who
is a slave, designated for another man but not
ransomed or given her freedom, an inquiry shall be
held. They shall be [put to death].*

Leviticus 19:20

All who curse father or mother shall be put to death ... If a man commits adultery with the wife of his neighbor, both the adulterer and the adulteress shall be put to death. The man who lies with his father's wife has uncovered his father's nakedness; both of them shall be put to death ... If a man lies with his daughter-in-law, both of them shall be put to death ... If a man lies with a male as with a woman, both of them have committed an abomination; they shall be put to death ... If a man takes a wife and her mother also, it is depravity; they shall be burned to death, both he and they ... If a man has sexual relations with an animal, he shall be put to death, and you shall kill the animal. If a woman approaches any animal and has sexual relations with it, you shall kill the woman and the animal. A man or a woman who is a medium or a wizard shall be put to death; they shall be stoned to death, their blood is upon them.

Leviticus 20:9-16

When the daughter of a priest profanes herself through prostitution, she profanes her father; she shall be burned to death.

Leviticus 21:9

One who blasphemes the name of the Lord shall be put to death; the whole congregation shall stone the blasphemer. Aliens as well as citizens, when they blaspheme the Name, shall be put to death.

Leviticus 24:16

Today, it is inconceivable to believe that a person deserves to be executed for any of these offenses. Isn't it odd that the stigma of a homosexual act still lingers? We should note that this applied only to male homosexual acts. As far as the Hebrew scriptures are concerned, lesbian acts are not a problem. Since women were not exempt from other sexual regulations, there is no reason to assume this is just an oversight.

Again, in the Levitical Holiness Code, the foremost concern with male homosexual acts was that it was imperative for the Hebrews to have children. Almost as significant was that the people of God not commit acts linked to the abominations that the fertility religions of the region committed. The fact that lesbian acts were spared any condemnation shows that the writers' concern regarding male same-sex acts was rooted only in those dual realities.

Modern Christians, when asked how they can eat pork when the Bible expressly forbids it, are prone to explain that Christ has set us free from the law. That is also how the apostle Paul explained it. Why, then, have we not also been freed from the Levitical law concerning male homosexual acts?

Now, back to my point about translation and interpretation. Compare the common translation of Leviticus 20:13 with a literal, word-for-word translation. It is commonly translated:

> *If a man lies with a male as with a woman, both of them have committed an abomination.*

The Hebrew actually says:

> *Two men must not engage in sexual activity on a woman's bed; it is ritually unclean.*

So guys, stay off your mother's bed.

It is obvious from this literal translation that what we read in our Bibles is not only a translation, but also an interpretation. You interpret it every time you read it. So do I. So does anyone who might want to use it as a weapon against you or someone you love.

Sodom

Out of the thousands of verses in the Hebrew scripture, there is only one other passage that deserves mention. That's because this story has been one of the most abused and misused passages in the Bible. I am talking, of course, about the story of Sodom, found in the book of Genesis. In using this story to condemn homosexuality, however, fundamentalists often commit the very acts for which God judged Sodom. In their rush to force the story to support their prejudices, they miss the real point.

There is a great deal that could be said about this story, but people only need to read it for themselves. Even a superficial reading clearly shows that the inhabitants of Sodom were a violent and abusive people who violated the basic hospitality codes needed for survival in that region.

Two angels or, more accurately, messengers from God were sent to the city of Sodom. Their objective was to warn Lot, Abraham and Sarah's son-in-law, that the city of Sodom was going to be destroyed. According to the story, "every single man in Sodom, both young and old," gathered outside Lot's home and insisted that he send these two visitors/strangers out.

Genesis 19:5 is the key verse in this passage. The New Revised Standard Version (NRSV) of the Bible translates it, "And they called to Lot, 'Where are the men who came to you tonight? Bring them out to us, so that we may know them.'" The Jerusalem Bible says, "Send them out to us so that we may abuse them." The New International Version renders that phrase "that we might have sex with them."

Those three very different translations are an example of the longstanding confusion over this passage. They also indicate that, in each case, the translators were reflecting their own personal biases. Was the original writer really suggesting that every man in Sodom wanted to have sex with these two strangers? Probably not.

In that day, homosexual rape was often a way for conquerors to degrade and devalue a vanquished foe. There is no basis for comparing the proposed abuse of the strangers with loving acts between consenting adults. To condemn homosexuality on the basis of this story would be as irrational as condemning heterosexuality on the basis of the rape of Tamar found in II Samuel 13:1-33.

Whether what they were proposing to do to Lot's guests was heterosexual rape or homosexual rape really does not matter. The point is that God finds abuse of any people repugnant. The lesson for modern Christians is that people in power who abuse those who are vulnerable infuriate the God of Jesus Christ.

Interestingly, I have yet to hear fundamentalists condemn Lot's offering his own virgin daughters to these vile and abusive Sodomites. Somehow, the self-righteous have considered that aspect less reprehensible than their own interpretation that the men of Sodom might have wanted to have sex with the male visitors. Rape of Lot's young daughters seems to be regarded as a legitimate alternative. The wonder is not that God destroyed Sodom, but that God did not include Lot in that destruction.

One easily could argue that the gay-bashers and homophobic hate-mongers are the real Sodomites of society today. They are the ones who consistently abuse the "strangers" in their midst. Their guilt is even clearer when we read what Ezekiel 16:48-49 says the sin of Sodom really was:

*As I live, says the Lord God, your sister Sodom
and her daughters have not done as you and your
daughters have done. This was the guilt of your
sister Sodom: she and her daughters were haughty,
overfed, rich and lazy, but did not assist the poor
and needy.*

Could it be that self-righteous people find it more
comfortable to conclude that God annihilated Sodom for
deeds they have not committed than for the deeds of which
they have been guilty? Could it be that it is more reassuring
to believe that Sodomites perished because of homosexuality
than because they were "haughty, overfed, rich and lazy"
and because "they did not assist the poor and needy"?
I had to laugh aloud once when a San Antonio-based
television preacher again linked the destruction of Sodom
to homosexuality. The preacher, who was significantly
overweight, needs to read the whole testimony of scripture.
Hebrew writings linked being overfed to Sodom much more
specifically than being gay. In that day, being overfed meant
consuming more than one's share of resources. That was
sinful because it was unhealthy and because the majority of
the world went to bed hungry every night.

Furthermore, Jesus clearly saw Sodom as a place that
was guilty of inhospitality to strangers. Luke 10:10-12 says:

*But whenever you enter a town and they do not
receive you, go into the streets and say, "Even the
dust of your town that clings to our feet, we wipe
off against you; nevertheless know this, that the
kingdom of God has come near." I tell you, it shall
be more tolerable on that day for Sodom than for
that town.*

Although Jesus condemned the violent treatment of

visitors by the residents of Sodom, he conspicuously avoided using the story to condemn any sexual behavior. As any first-year psychology major knows, rape is not about sex; it is about power, abuse and violence. Whether the violence is done to a woman, a man, a child or an angel, it is loathsome to God. Whether homosexuals or heterosexuals commit the act, it is sinful.

I think that would include the violence of gay-bashing that is epidemic in this country. That kind of treatment is often rationalized in the same dehumanizing terms with which the Religious Right refers to lesbians and gay men. Those who verbally, mentally, spiritually and physically abuse people who are different or are strangers are the real Sodomites of our day. Cloaking the abuse in religious language does not make it acceptable to God.

The Christian Scripture

As we move from the Hebrew scripture to the Christian scripture, we proceed pretty quickly, since the New Testament contains few passages that are directly relevant to homosexuality. The Gospels that contain the words of Jesus have nothing negative to say about lesbians or gays. That alone should be enough to cause any thoughtful Christian to pause and wonder what the big deal is if Jesus never spoke one word about it. If Jesus did not find love between two people of the same sex offensive, then one must wonder why it creates such problems for so many fundamentalist Christians today. Clearly, their discomfort points to their own insecurity and fear rather than to any spiritual reality based in the life and teachings of Jesus. Although Jesus **never** said, or even implied, **anywhere** in the Gospels that a person's sexuality or sexual orientation was in any way a factor in his or her relationship with God, He did:

- criticize, repeatedly, those who self-righteously judge and condemn;
- talk of his efforts to bring the ostracized sheep from other flocks into God's fold;
- violate many social taboos of his day.

The beautiful Bible verse that begins "God so loved the world" is often quoted by evangelical Christians, but it is not followed by conditions or qualifiers that limit that love to the heterosexuals of the world.

Ancient Greek culture, which disdained the physical side of life as inferior, has strongly influenced the Church. As a result of that Neo-Platonic influence, as interpreted through persons like Augustine and Aquinas, the Church historically has been a sex-negative institution. It is a tragedy and a heresy that human sexuality and spirituality have become such separate parts of our lives that they seldom intersect. It is little wonder that fundamentalist Christians struggle so deeply with the sexuality and spirituality of people who are different, since they seem totally incapable of reconciling their own sexuality and faith. Both of these parts of our lives are beautiful gifts of a loving God.

In the early 1970s, a friend, who was youth director at a Baptist church, was discharged from his job. Church administrators fired him after one of his students timidly asked if people who masturbated went to hell. My friend said they did not and explained how sex was a sacred gift from God that one should use responsibly. Later that week, the deacon who informed him of his termination said quite pointedly, "This church believes that Sunday School is no place for kids to learn about sex." When he asked the deacon just where they were supposed to learn, since most kids were never taught at home, the deacon replied that he thought they should learn on the streets like "normal kids."

How sad that the Church is still so shame-filled about

the God-given gift of human sexuality. Undoubtedly, shame is not a part of the teachings of Jesus. He said nothing to cause lesbian and gay people to feel alienated from God, and Jesus said nothing that should make heterosexuals ashamed of their sexuality either. Sex is not some dirty secret about which we must keep God ignorant.

In the Christian scriptures, there are a couple of passages in the writings of Paul that we should explore. First, we should note that, like the writer of Leviticus, Paul was influenced by contemporary culture. A classic example is found in 1 Corinthians 11:11-15. Paul wrote to the people in Corinth, saying that men should have short hair, while women's hair should be long. This teaching had a purely cultural basis and was irrelevant to any other people, even of Paul's day. I remember growing up in the 1960s and hearing preachers quote Paul to prove that long hair on men or boys was sinful.

The passages of Paul's writings that refer to specific homosexual behaviors are very similar. Romans 1:26-32 and 1 Corinthians 6:9 are the two New Testament passages most commonly wielded against lesbian and gay Christians. Again, there are a number of books that deal with these passages more comprehensively than we can do here. Robin Scroggs' book *The New Testament and Homosexuality* is an excellent treatise of this subject. John Boswell's *Christianity, Social Tolerance, and Homosexuality* also has become a classic. However, books like these are sometimes a bit inaccessible for persons without theological training. It is important that we not discard the scriptures because of a couple of passages fundamentalists have used to bash us. Such use is completely the opposite of the Apostle Paul's original intention.

The primary point in dealing with these passages is to understand that Paul was never referring to homosexual love as we know it. What he saw was the behavior of the Roman world in which he lived. The Greek words that he used make it clear that the activity Paul found immoral was associated with idolatry and the worship of pagan gods and goddesses. The apostle wrote during the time of people like Nero, who had two of his wives executed. Nero then became enamored of a young boy who looked like his second wife. He had the boy castrated and then married him in a public ceremony. It was a time when male and female temple prostitutes, and older men with young boys, committed the most visible homosexual acts.

Paul, whose command of the Greek language was quite good, never used the Greek word for homosexuality. In fact, that word never appears in the Bible. Instead, the words he used refer to the specific behavior that I have just described. If we could read and understand what Paul wrote in the original language and context, few lesbian or gay people would disagree with him. Let's look at those passages:

> *For this reason God gave them up to degrading passions. Their women exchanged natural intercourse for unnatural, and in the same way also the men, giving up natural intercourse with women, were consumed with passion for one another. Men committed shameless acts with men and received in their own persons the due penalty for their error.*
>
> Romans 1:26-27

As you can see, this passage picks up in the middle of a thought: "For this reason." For what reason? That is the point so often overlooked in studying scripture. To deal with this passage fairly, it is essential that the reading begin at verse 16. No one should dare omit the basic premise of verse 17 that "the righteous live by faith," not by their good works, their church membership or their sexual orientation.

God makes us righteous by our faith. Paul summarizes for us again in Romans 3:23-24. He writes, "All have sinned and fallen short of the glory of God; we are then justified by God's grace as a gift, through the redemption that is in Christ Jesus." Although the fundamentalists may forget this concept, we need to always keep in mind that God reconciles us by Christ Jesus, not by our sexuality.

Now, in Romans 1:18, Paul begins to describe the ungodliness of those who have chosen the path of wickedness. In the context of such, he describes women who "exchanged natural intercourse for unnatural" and men who also gave up natural intercourse with women and "were consumed with passion for one another." He concludes, in verse 29, with a list of offenses, such as covetousness, malice, envy, murder, strife, deceit, craftiness, gossip, slander, insolence, haughtiness, boasting, inventing evil, rebelling against parents, foolishness, and being heartless or ruthless.

This is the only passage in the whole Bible whose interpretation is a condemnation of lesbians. It seems that the apostle saw these people as heterosexuals who committed "unnatural acts." It is most likely that Paul witnessed these acts in the lives of those who worshiped pagan gods through the temple prostitution that was common in that day.

What Paul also seems to be trying to do with this passage is to take an "obvious" sinner, like one who worships through prostitution, and to hold them up as an example of someone who needs the redemption of God through Jesus Christ. Paul then goes on to list all of the "awful" deeds these "sinners" commit. Slyly, he includes in the list things of which every person is guilty, like gossip, haughtiness and foolishness. Soon, we are all hooked. Like the "obvious" sinner, we all stand in need of grace because we have all "sinned and come short of the glory of God."

It is important to note that what Paul was identifying as evil was activity he saw as "unnatural." For lesbians or gay men, pretending to be heterosexual is a violation of their nature and would qualify as an unnatural act. It is deceit, a manifestation of one of the very transgressions Paul highlighted as wicked. The evil of living a lie is obvious to all who have tried to do so. It leaves the pretender dehumanized and broken, and it rends the very fabric of creation itself. It also makes authentic relationships impossible. This includes our relationship with God.

In one Methodist church where I was the associate pastor the senior minister casually mentioned in one morning's sermon that "nature itself demonstrates that homosexuality is wrong." At that time in my life, I did not argue the point, even in the privacy of my mind. Later that week, I stopped by the pastor's house, and we visited for a few minutes in the front yard. He noticed I was looking over his shoulder and not paying attention to what he was saying. Turning around, he saw I was watching his German shepherd humping his black Labrador. He said, "Yeah, they do that all the time."

"Oh?" I said pointedly, "I thought they were both females."

From dogs to dolphins, same-gender sexual attraction is a reality. What is "natural" for one individual may be a direct violation of another's nature. We, who God has created, have an obligation to live out, as fully as possible, the nature with which God created us. To do otherwise is unhealthy and an insult to God.

> *Do you not know that wrongdoers will not inherit the kingdom of God? Do not be deceived! Fornicators, idolaters, adulterers, male prostitutes, sodomites, thieves, greedy, drunkards, revilers, robbers; none of these will inherit the kingdom of God.*
>
> 1 Corinthians 6:9-10

This means understanding that the law is laid down not for the innocent but for the lawless and disobedient, for the godless and sinful, for the unholy and profane, for those who kill their father or mother, for murderers, fornicators, sodomites, slave traders, liars, perjurers, and whatever else is contrary to the sound teaching.

1 Timothy 1:9-10

Both of these passages are favorites of fundamentalists. The word translated above as "sodomites" by the NRSV was translated by the King James Version as "effeminate" and "abusers of themselves with mankind." The Revised Standard Version (RSV) was the first to render both of the words simply and erroneously "homosexuals." The tragic implication of the RSV translation was that it made the passage say that persons who were attracted to people of the same sex were excluded from the "kingdom of God" in the same way as murderers or slave traders might be. The New International Version translates the words "male prostitutes" and "homosexual offenders." The New Jerusalem Bible translates the words "catamites" and "sodomites." Ironically, the footnotes to I Corinthians 6:9-10 in the Third Oxford Edition of the NRSV note:

The Greek terms translated "male prostitutes" and "sodomites" do not refer to homosexuals as in inappropriate older translations.

Nowhere does the author use the traditional Greek word for homosexual. The word that translates as "catamite" is usually used to refer to youth that exchanged sexual favors for money from older men. In their book *Is the Homosexual My Neighbor?*, Virginia Mollenkott and Letha Scanzoni suggested that the second word translated "sodomite" might also mean "obsessive corruptor of boys." What Paul seems to be condemning is the practice, common in that day, of older men using adolescent boys for sexual purposes in exchange for educating them or giving them large sums of money. In other words, he is denouncing boy prostitutes and their customers.

While this passage may not speak of homosexual relationships, what does seem worthy of our concern today is the practice of sexual exploitation. The Cathedral of Hope opened a shelter for homeless teenagers whose parents, disapproving of their children's sexual orientations, threw them out of their homes. For these young people, then and now, prostitution was, perhaps, their only option for staying alive. Several "charitable" homeless shelters refuse to accept young adults who are known to be gay.

Paul is not excluding people who are lesbian or gay as we understand them today from the realm of God. Again, Biblical writers, including Paul, had no understanding of this psychosexual orientation with which a person is born. At most, he was condemning sexual practices of which he disapproved. We should also note that, today, we contextualize or recognize as incorrect many of Paul's teachings. For example, the Apostle Paul:

- believed no one should marry because Jesus would return in his lifetime;
- encouraged slaves to simply obey their masters;
- taught that women should be submissive and obedient to men;
- taught that women should not teach men.

Many of Paul's teachings on these subjects are much more extensive than the few disputed verses referring to certain homosexual actions.

The Protestant Bible is divided into 66 books. Those

books are divided into 1,189 chapters. Those chapters are made up of 31,173 verses. Of those, only five verses even remotely refer to certain homosexual acts. There is no doubt that anyone reading the Bible in its entirety and without the disadvantage of cultural bias would regard a person's sexuality as of little consequence to God. Why, then, is it so consequential to fundamentalist Christianity?

Could it be that any legalistic, religious scheme requires having someone whose sins are more severe? Is the fundamentalists' need to be right so great that it justifies Biblical distortion? Only those Christians can answer that conclusively, but the Bible clearly does not support their condemnation of lesbian and gay Christians. Is it just coincidental that the rise in the condemnation of the so called "gay agenda" coincided with the demise of the specter of communism? There needs to be someone to fear or hate if religious organizations are going to raise large sums of money. Racism, the "Red Scare" and "the Evil Empire" seem to have been replaced by homosexuals. The fear-mongering of homophobia has filled the emotional gap left by the demise of the acceptability of public racism. A system of beliefs that requires someone who is a greater sinner than we are does not rely very confidently on the grace of God.

I was born and raised Episcopalian, sampled the Baptist church and Southern Baptist Convention while in college, and came to the Cathedral of Hope after not being able to find an Episcopal church which was a good fit when I moved to Dallas in 1995. I had never experienced that kind of "welling up" of feelings, the certain knowledge that "God is in this place" until then. I have never shed tears of sorrow or tears of such incredible joy than those shed at CoH. I have never felt such a swell in my breast than when seeing the hands uplifted, uniting one with another giving thanks after Communion at CoH. What a message that sends to heaven and back again!

I have never felt that my giving to special needs went to better use than when giving to Thanksgiving baskets, or Christmas Angels, or Loaves and Fishes, or school supplies and uniforms, or even just praying daily for needs coming in from all over the world. As Mother Teresa said so profoundly, "Let them see what we do." This gay church is a congregation who "puts its money where its mouth is" in terms of service and giving back to the community, and that's where I found Jesus.

Sara Sprecher
Dallas, Texas

Chapter 3
The Bible as a Shield

Words of Hope and Help for Lesbian and Gay People

We have concluded that, while the Bible does condemn certain homosexual acts within specific contexts, it also condemns certain heterosexual acts. However, it does not condemn either homosexuality or heterosexuality as a whole. The next step, then, is to ask if the Bible has anything positive to say to us as lesbian or gay Christians. Of course, it does. The Bible reveals and teaches us about the God of creation, redemption and resurrection. The Bible is filled with many lessons that are just as valuable to lesbian and gay Christians as they are to heterosexual Christians.

More importantly, we need to ask if the Bible speaks directly to the unique situation of lesbian and gay people today. Obviously, it does not speak of the modern lesbian/gay lifestyle any more than the Bible speaks of contemporary Latino culture or of recent African-American history. However, that is not to say that there are no stories or teachings that are especially relevant.

Indeed, we find a story of a struggling, single mother who finds solace in a covenant relationship with another woman. In another story, we see a father who becomes outraged when he discovers that his son has become involved with another man, but the relationship between the son and the other man survives because it is based on a commitment of love.

Same-Sex Love

Numerous passages in the Bible speak tenderly of love between two people of the same gender. The best known, of course, are the stories of Ruth and Naomi and of Jonathan and David. People of both the Hebrew and Christian faiths have long honored these relationships. Although all four of these people had heterosexual relationships, scriptures very powerfully record and revere their love for a person of the same gender. Let's start with the story of Ruth and Naomi and see what it might say to us.

Ruth and Naomi

The book of Ruth begins with the story of a woman named Naomi. Because of a famine, Naomi was forced to move to Moab with her husband and two sons. Although she found food there, she also found great grief in Moab. First, her husband died, and Naomi was left with two boys. Eventually, the sons of Naomi married women from Moab, but, after about 10 years, they, too, died without fathering children.

There is no explanation for the deaths of these three men, but the grief Naomi felt must have been overwhelming. Not only had she lost three people she loved, but the outlook was grim for a woman of that day who was left without a husband or sons. Begging and prostitution were the most common options for a woman without a husband, children or grandchildren. In addition, she found herself in a foreign land.

Jeanette Foster, in her book *Sex Variant Women in Literature*, writes about the subtleties of the lives of women in the Bible that male scholars too often have missed. She suggests that the Book of Ruth might have been written by a woman since it focuses on the life of two women, Naomi and Ruth. There is no external evidence of that, but there is no evidence a man wrote it either. We see a great deal of compassion shown for the situation in which Naomi and her daughters-in-law found themselves. Such compassion for women was not typical of male writers of that day, who regarded women as little more than property.

We find no indication that the deaths of Naomi's three loved ones were blamed on some sin they, or she, might have committed. They are simply reported as the tragic results of the rain falling on the just and the unjust. The only sin presented in this story is that Naomi, who was the victim of a tragedy, now became the victim of an unjust and sexist society that systematically deprived women of basic human rights. This is a sin that lingers to this day.

For Naomi, the retribution for sexism might well have cost her life. She lived not far from where women, even today, are abused and left to starve. With that perspective, Naomi decided that her best hope would be to leave Moab and return to her hometown of Bethlehem. Let's pick the story up in Ruth 1:6-13:

> *Then Naomi started to return with her daughters-in-law from the country of Moab, for she had heard in the country of Moab that the Lord had considered the people and given them food. So she set out from the place where she had been living, she and her two daughters-in-law, and they went on their way to go back to the land of Judah. But Naomi said to her two daughters-in-law, "Go back each of you to your mother's house. May the Lord deal kindly with you, as you have dealt with the dead and with me. The Lord grant that you may find security, each of you in the house of your husband." Then she kissed them, and they wept aloud. They said to her, "No, we will return*

with you to your people." Naomi replied, "No my
daughters, it has been far more bitter for me than
for you, because the hand of the Lord has turned
against me."

Naomi heard that her hometown of Bethlehem once again had food. The famine was over; she could go home again. She and the two younger women packed up their few personal belongings and set out. Along the way, Naomi decided that it would be best for these two women to do exactly what she was doing. Although she had lost everything else, she decided it was unfair for her to cling to Ruth and Orpah and ruin what was left of their lives. Putting aside her own pain and need, Naomi tried to send them off to their own families where they would have a better chance of starting over.

When we are in pain and struggling with a sense of loss, it is easy to become so consumed by that struggle that we forget the needs of those around us. That is why, in the midst of AIDS and in the middle of a war with the Religious Right, it is imperative that lesbian and gay Christians remember that there are others who also have needs. In order for us to stay spiritually healthy, we, like Naomi, must be able to look beyond our personal needs and struggles to help someone else. Perhaps if we are feeling overwhelmed right now, the best thing we could do is to find someone else who is hurting or struggling and try to help them.

In addition to that bit of self-help insight, there is an interesting piece of theology in this passage. Notice that Naomi is trying to send away both daughters-in-law. Orpah listens to her former mother-in-law and goes, but Ruth insists on staying with Naomi. What might have happened if Naomi had been more persuasive and insistent, or if Ruth's love for her had been less tenacious? The major point of the book of Ruth is that Ruth, a foreigner, becomes an ancestor of great King David and of his even greater descendant Jesus. If Ruth had returned to Moab as Naomi suggests, that might never have happened.

This reality opens all sorts of questions and should remind us to be aware of just how powerful every choice we make might be. Ruth never knew that she was used by God in such a powerful way, but her decision made a major difference in the history of Israel and the world.

At any rate, there is no voice from heaven that tried to stop Naomi from sending them away nor to stop Ruth from going. Apparently, all that keeps that from happening is Ruth's love for Naomi. Ironic, isn't it, that one woman's love for another leads to a series of events through which God redeems humanity? It should not be surprising since the most famous passage in the book of Ruth, and one of the most famous passages in the Bible, is the pledge of love between these two women:

> *Ruth said, "Do not press me to leave you or to turn back from following you! Where you go, I will go; Where you lodge, I will lodge; your people shall be my people, and your God my God. Where you die, I will die; there will I be buried. May the Lord do thus and so to me, and more as well, if even death parts me from you!" When Naomi saw she was determined to go with her, she said no more to her.*
> Ruth 1:16-18

For lesbian and gay people, this passage is important for a number of reasons. It has always been honored as a classic statement of love and fidelity. Ministers have read this passage thousands of times at weddings, but I have never once heard it noted during a heterosexual wedding that these words were spoken by one woman to another woman whom she loved.

I do, however, recall a wedding that I did many years ago as a United Methodist pastor in which the bride insisted we use this text. The problem was that when I read these words, the maid-of-honor dropped her flowers and ran from the room wailing. I had no idea what was wrong with the poor woman. It wasn't until years later that I finally put it together. These women were the best of friends, they loved to go camping together, they were the best softball players on our church team ... I've always wondered what happened to those two.

If the author of the book of Ruth was a man, he probably recorded these words with no more awareness of their full meaning than I had on that day during that wedding years ago. If, however, the author of the book of Ruth was a woman, it is possible that she understood precisely what was happening here. She would have known that, although they were almost utterly dependent on men for their physical survival, women of that day often turned to one another for the tenderness, affection and companionship they longed for and needed. Notice, in verse 14, how the author recorded Ruth clinging to Naomi. This physical point of contact had probably become an important part of their survival in the face of brutal sexism and personal grief.

As far as I know, Jeanette Foster is almost the only scholar who dares to suggest that the relationship between Ruth and Naomi was sexual. The idea of sex being a part of a relationship between two women is not something that would occur to the average male Biblical scholar. Combine sexism and homophobia and you have a most powerful silencer. Why wouldn't their love have found intimate expression? And if it didn't, was their love lessened?

In Dr. Tom Horner's book *Jonathan Loved David* there is an interesting chapter on Ruth and Naomi. Horner, an Episcopal priest, observes that in the Middle East women spend almost all of their time with other women. If they had become sexually or affectionately involved with one another, their husbands would not likely have noticed or cared unless it interfered with their dinner.

Interestingly, in Ruth 1:17, Ruth vows:

> *Where you die, I will die—there will I be buried.*
> *May the Lord do thus and so to me, and more as*
> *well, if even death parts me from you!*

The words "the Lord do thus and so to me, and more" would have accompanied a gesture of some sort to indicate what kind of punishment she hoped Yahweh would visit upon her if she broke this vow. The gesture might have been a chopping motion on an arm or the side of the neck. It was as serious a vow as a Jew would accept, since they could not swear by Yahweh's name. Notice, when we get to 1 Samuel 20:13, Jonathan says to his beloved David:

> *But if my father intends to do you harm, the Lord*
> *do so to me, and more also, if I do not disclose it to*
> *you, and send you away, so you may go in safety.*

In her vow, Ruth says that she is willing to leave her people and her faith. That is more than just the love of a daughter-in-law for her mother-in-law. Her vow is as deep and profound an expression of committed love as can be found anywhere. Her willingness to risk everything tells of her devotion and of the kind of person Naomi must have been. What did Ruth find in this Hebrew woman that made her determined to give up her people and her god in order to embrace the Jewish people and Yahweh as her God?

Chapter one ends with Ruth in Naomi's arms making a powerful vow of love. The point of all of this is not to prove that Ruth and Naomi were lesbians or lovers, but to register, very clearly, on our consciousness the sacred quality of love expressed between two people of the same gender. Unfortunately, because of the social structure of their day, these women would still need a man to help them if they were to survive.

Ruth met Boaz, an older man and distant relative of her dead husband, and, together, they had a son they named Obed. He became the ancestor of great King David and, ultimately, of Jesus. Even after she married, however, Ruth did not abandon Naomi. They continued to live together, and Naomi served as a nursemaid for the new baby. There is an interesting passage in Ruth 4:14-15:

> *Then the women said to Naomi, "Blessed be the Lord, who has not left you this day without next-of-kin; and may his name be renowned in Israel! He shall be to you a restorer of life and a nourisher of your old age; for your daughter-in-law who loves you, who is more to you than seven sons, has borne him."*

Even after the birth of a son, the community of women recognized that Ruth's love and care for her former mother-in-law surpassed the kind of care that Naomi would have gotten if she had seven sons and seven daughters-in-law. What an amazing tribute to their love, but I have never heard a sermon on that text. Its neglect has diminished our faith and our relationships.

This story reminds those of us in same-sex relationships that the love we pledge can endure because it is sacred in God's eyes. Whether Ruth and Naomi had sexual relations is of little consequence to this point.

It seems that heterosexuals are the ones who seem so obsessed with the sex lives of lesbians and gays. I do not think that even the most energetic of us spend more than 1 percent of our week having sex. The other 99 percent is spent working and sleeping, loving and fighting, struggling and growing, dreaming and hoping. Like Ruth, we make our commitments to one another:

- **Entreat me not to leave you**: I'm not going anywhere. You can relax. I have made my commitment, and I am here to stay.
- **Where you go, I will go**: I know life is uncertain, and, sometimes, we will have to move or change or go in a different direction. That's okay. My love for you is real, and if you have to go, then I'll go, too.
- **Where you lodge I will lodge**: We are going to live together. That means we'll share a bed and toothpaste. I'll have to eat food you like, and you'll have to eat food I like. We're going to work out our differences here in this home.
- **Your people will be my people**: We are family, and, though it may be a challenge, your family will be my family.
- **Your God will be my God**: We will share the same faith and the same values. God will make our relationship strong.
- **May the Lord do so to me and more also if anything but death parts you from me**: This is not a commitment I will keep only as long as I am in the mood or until something better comes along. It is my life I'm committing to you.

Ruth kept her vow. Although she married Boaz in order to survive, she never broke her vow to Naomi. This story is a reminder to us that people of the same sex can make vows to each other that God recognizes, sanctifies and honors. Those vows are just as strong, just as powerful and just as important as vows made by persons of different genders.

I once heard that the average marriage in America lasts seven years, and that is with all the legal and social support of our society compelling the couple to stay together. Imagine how much lower that average would go if we factored in all those relationships where heterosexuals made commitments to each other but never got married, or emotionally left the relationship without getting a divorce.

To imply that same-sex relationships cannot endure is simply wrong. They can and do. We must, however, make sure that we reserve the kinds of vows that Ruth made only for people we have known long enough to be certain it is a vow we can keep. In the end, the part of the vow that includes God is the strongest asset any relationship can have, regardless of our sexual orientation.

In three decades of pastoring, I have never had anyone tell me that their partnership failed if they believed God led them together and if they prayed for their relationship every day. If you want your relationship to last forever, then make promises that you have every intention of keeping and ask God every day to help you keep them. We are only responsible for our side of the relationship, but when we really take care of our side, the other side usually takes care of itself.

Jonathan and David

The Bible tells us that David was a man after God's own heart. He was the greatest king Israel has ever had. As a mere boy, he courageously faced and defeated the overgrown Philistine named Goliath. When Jonathan, the son of King Saul, heard David telling his father about the conflict with the giant, Jonathan immediately fell in love with David and gave him his robe, armor and even his weapons:

When David had finished speaking to Saul, the soul of Jonathan was bound to the soul of David, and Jonathan loved him as his own soul. Saul took him that day and would not let him return to his father's house. Then Jonathan made a covenant with David, because he loved him as his own soul. Jonathan stripped himself of the robe that he was wearing, and gave it to David, along with his armor, and even his sword and his bow and his belt.

1 Samuel 18:1-4

David's skill as a musician enabled him to bring relief to the tormented mind of King Saul; thus, he came to live in the palace with his friend, the son of his king. Later, as Saul's mental condition deteriorated, Saul came to see David as a threat and repeatedly tried to kill him. Jonathan, however, loved David "as his own soul" and continually rescued him. What we have here is a painful picture of a man caught between his loyalty to his father and his love of another man.

Dr. Horner answers the critics who say, "But can't two men just be friends?"

But when the two men come from a society that for 200 years had lived in the shadow of the Philistine culture which accepted homosexuality; when one of them — who is the social superior of the two — publicly makes a display of his love (1 Samuel 18:3-4); when the two of them make a lifetime pact openly (1 Samuel 20:16-17); when they meet secretly and kiss each other and shed copious tears at parting (1 Samuel 20:41); when one of them proclaims that his love for the other surpassed his love for women (2 Samuel 1:26) — and all of this is present in the David and Jonathan liaison — we have every reason to believe that a homosexual relationship existed.

Horner goes on to suggest that the only thing left to confirm this assumption is a parent who is furious over the relationship, and King Saul is that. When he learned that Jonathan was aiding and abetting David, he said to him:

> *You son of a perverse, rebellious woman! Do I not know that you have chosen the son of Jesse to your own shame, and to the shame of your mother's nakedness? For as long as the son of Jesse lives upon the earth, neither you nor your kingdom shall be established. Now bring him to me, for he shall surely die.*
>
> 1 Samuel 20:30-31

Truly, Saul sounds like a modern fundamentalist father who has just discovered that his son loves another man. He begins by blaming Jonathan's state, first, on Jonathan's mother. He uses the word "pervert." Saul speaks of his son's nakedness and shame and then projects the shame onto Jonathan's mother, but the real humiliation filled Saul's demented heart. He interpreted Jonathan's love for David as an action that would destroy Jonathan's bright future. Jonathan, however, seemed quite content to let the friend he loved take the place that might have otherwise been his. His love for David exceeded his ambition for the throne of Israel. This is no mere buddy.

In his article "Same-Sex Relationships in the Bible," found on religoustolerance.org, B. A. Robinson makes an interesting observation about 1 Samuel 18:20-21:

> *Now Saul's daughter Michal was in love with David, and when they told Saul about it, he was*

pleased. "I will give her to him," he thought, "so that she may be a snare to him and so that the hand of the Philistines may be against him." Now you have a second opportunity to become my son-in-law.
New International Version

In the King James Version, the end of Verse 21 reads:

Thou shalt this day be my son-in-law, in the one of the twain.

Saul's belief was that David would be so distracted by a wife that he would not be an effective fighter and would be killed by the Philistines. He offered first his daughter Merab, but that was rejected, presumably by her. Then he offered Michal. There is an interesting phrase used at the end of verse 21. In both the New International Version and the King James Version, it would seem that David's first opportunity to be a son-in-law was with the older daughter Merab and his second was with the younger daughter Michal. The KJV preserves the original text in its clearest form; it implies that David would become Saul's son-in-law through "one of the twain." "Twain" means "two," so the verse seems to refer to one of Saul's two daughters. Unfortunately, this is a mistranslation. The phrase "the one of" does not exist in the Hebrew original. The words are shown in italics in the King James Version; this is an admission by the translators that they made the words up. Thus, if the KJV translators had been truly honest, they would have written:

Thou shalt this day be my son-in-law, in the twain.

In modern English, this might be written, "Today, you are son-in-law with two of my children." That would refer to both his son Jonathan and his daughter Michal.

The Hebrew original would appear to recognize David and Jonathan's homosexual relationship as equivalent to David and Michal's heterosexual marriage. Saul may have approved or disapproved of the same-sex relationship, but, at least, he appears to have recognized it. The translators of the KJV highlight their re-writing of the Hebrew original by placing the three words in italics; the NIV translation is clearly deceptive.

There is no question that both men were married to women and each fathered children. The question has never been whether the Bible records any honorable relationships between men and women, but how the Bible treats relationships between persons of the same gender. When, how, or even if David and Jonathan's love was sexually expressed is really not the point. Both the Bible and history have honored their passionate love for one another. The sex life of David and Jonathan is almost inconsequential. It is the passion of the love they share that really matters. Jonathan and David's passion was so honored that it has been recorded and retold for thousands of years. There are very few loves about which we can say that.

Of even more importance than the passion of their relationship is their faithfulness to one another. On two different occasions, the Bible records Jonathan making a covenant with David. Their story is clearly a covenant of love, and it models for the world that two people of the same gender can, and do, make loving covenants that they keep and that keep them. It is important for lesbian and gay people to reclaim the power of sacred covenants for our lives—the kinds of covenants recorded in the Biblical books of Ruth and Samuel.

The Teachings of Jesus

We already have established that Jesus had nothing negative to say about lesbian and gay people, but is it possible that some of his teachings are especially relevant to us? We should examine two passages in particular. The first is found in Matthew 8:5-13.

In this story, a Roman centurion, seeking healing for one of his servants, comes to see Jesus. There are several remarkable aspects of this story. This gentile soldier's faith obviously impresses Jesus. He clearly understands some things about how faith works that the followers of Jesus were having trouble grasping. The other remarkable thing about this story is the compassion of the centurion. His concern for this "servant" is touching. He describes himself as "a man under authority." In other words, he is someone accustomed to giving orders and to being obeyed. He commanded both soldiers and servants, but here we find him going in person to seek the help of an itinerant Jewish rabbi.

It would not be hard to conclude that the servant who is the focus of his concern is no ordinary servant. The centurion's personal intervention makes it clear that he has a special interest in the recovery of the one who is sick. That interest may be clarified further for us by reading the text in the original Greek. The word translated as "servant" or "boy-servant" is the Greek word "pais." It can be translated simply "boy," though it is also the word that is used by a man of that day to speak of a young, intimate friend. Alone, the use of this word would prove little, but coupled with the centurion's investment of himself, his time and his prestige, one can only conclude that what we have here is more than just a master-servant relationship. Could it be that the centurion discouraged Jesus from coming to his home because he was aware of how the Jews of that day felt about relationships such as his?

Jesus does not turn away from this man and his love for his servant in disgust. Rather, Jesus holds him up as an example by saying, "Truly I tell you, I have not found such faith as this in all of Israel." (Matthew 8:10) What an extraordinary compliment. If there was any doubt that Jesus honored this man and his love for his sick friend, we have the fact that Jesus healed him to dispel that doubt. As lesbian and gay people can testify, Jesus was right. In the face of the homophobia of religion it takes great faith to keep coming to Jesus in service and worship.

The teachings of Jesus that are most important to us as lesbian and gay people are the parables of inclusion such as the Prodigal Son, the Lost Sheep, and the Lost Coin, each found in the 15th chapter of Luke. In these stories, Jesus describes God's passionate concern for those who were left out, lost or misplaced. Most of us are familiar with the story of the Prodigal Son and know that the point is the unconditional, embracing love of the father. In that same chapter, Jesus talks about a shepherd who goes in search of one lost sheep. While most of us would look for a lost asset, the shepherd, who represents God, does a very foolish thing. The shepherd leaves the 99 sheep to go in search of one. It is a poignant reminder of the almost foolish desperation God feels about anyone being left out. Then, in the story of the Lost Coin, the woman, who also represents God, works very hard to ensure none of the coins are lost.

Through those teachings, Jesus indicates that it is the passion of God that **everyone** be included in the family. The way in which Jesus lived his life testified to that as well. His treatment of people who were traditionally ostracized by religion demonstrated that he disdained exclusionary faith systems. He told stories in which Samaritans were heroes. He treated women with a level of respect unheard of in that day and held them up as models for men (e.g., the widow who gave her last mite has become the Christian model

of genuine generosity). One of the first people to whom
Jesus "came out" as the Christ was a Samaritan woman. A
reading of that story in John 4 shows that the woman herself
was surprised, even shocked. Why would this rabbi have
anything to do with a woman in public? A common prayer
of that day was for a man to give thanks that he had not
been born a woman, a Samaritan or a dog.

No message was more clear, powerful or consistent
than the reality that Jesus came to include those whom the
Church had excluded from the family of God. If we miss that
point, we have missed the most important revelation of God
in human history. The evangelical doctrine of salvation says
that God reconciles us by our faith in Jesus Christ. Anything
more than that, other than that, or beyond that is idolatry.
That includes sexual orientation.

Jesus said that in heaven we would no longer marry
nor be given in marriage. (Luke 20:35) Perhaps he was saying
that things like sexual orientation will be insignificant in
heaven. In a community of mutual love and respect, those
kinds of labels become irrelevant. Wouldn't it be nice if
we could make our world a bit more like heaven in that
regard?

The Eunuchs

Perhaps the situation in the Bible that most closely parallels
the lesbian and gay community is the story of the eunuch.
The Jewish faith disenfranchised eunuchs. They could not
enter into the inner courts of the temple but had to remain
in the court of the gentiles. Historically, there were three
kinds of eunuchs. Jesus mentioned this fact in Matthew
19:10-12. He was talking about marriage, and he mentioned
that, "Some eunuchs were born that way, others have been
made eunuchs, and still others choose to be eunuchs for the

Kingdom's sake."

Since the Jews saw procreation as the principle purpose of sexual relations, Jesus was saying that there are three types of people who do not reproduce:

- Those who were born without being sexually attracted to members of the opposite sex.
- Those captured as slaves who, as a result of castration or other physical abuse, could no longer reproduce.
- Those who chose to remain celibate for the sake of the Dominion of God.

We cannot read the words that Jesus spoke about eunuchs without noting that he did not use that moment as a chance to say anything negative about eunuchs or persons of differing sexual orientation. How different that seems from the pattern of so many modern preachers who never seem to miss an opportunity for gay-bashing. I suppose part of the difference is that Jesus did not have to use fear, division or self-righteousness to raise millions of dollars to fund a ministry empire.

In Acts 8 there is a very powerful story that centers on a eunuch:

> Then an angel of the Lord said to Philip, "Get up and go toward the south to the road that goes down from Jerusalem to Gaza." So he got up and went. Now there was an Ethiopian eunuch, a court official of Candace, the queen of the Ethiopians, in charge of her entire treasury. He had come to Jerusalem to worship and was returning home; seated in his chariot, he was reading the prophet Isaiah. Then the Spirit said to Philip, "Go over to this chariot and join it." So Philip ran up to it and heard him reading

the prophet Isaiah. He asked, "Do you understand
what you are reading?" He replied, "How can I,
unless someone guides me?" And he invited Philip
to get in and sit beside him. Now the passage of the
scripture that he was reading was this: "Like a sheep
he was led to the slaughter, and like a lamb silent
before its shearer, so he does not open his mouth. In
his humiliation justice was denied him. Who can
describe his generation? For his life is taken away
from the earth." The eunuch asked Philip, "About
whom, may I ask you, does the prophet say this,
about himself or about someone else?" Then Philip
began to speak, and starting with this scripture, he
proclaimed to him the good news about Jesus. As
they were going along the road, they came to some
water; and the eunuch said, "Look, here is water!
What is to prevent me from being baptized?" He
commanded the chariot to stop, and both of them,
Philip and the eunuch, went down into the water,
and Philip baptized him. When they came up out
of the water, the Spirit of the Lord snatched Philip
away; the eunuch saw him no more, and went on
his way rejoicing.*

Acts 8:26-39

In this story, God sent Philip, one of the original
deacons, to share his faith with a man from Ethiopia who
was riding in a chariot reading from the book of Isaiah. The
eunuch was the treasurer of Candace, Queen of Ethiopia.

It was the custom of that day that captors of men or
boys would enslave them and often castrate them, generally
by removing only the testicles. This was done to keep slaves
from reproducing, as well as a means to subjugate a man
by literally emasculating him. It should be noted, however,
that castrated men do not become homosexual, nor do they

always lose their sex drive. Therefore, those slaves who served the queen or the women of the royal family were not just castrated slaves. When it came to those of the royal households, they were not only afraid that a woman of the royal house might become pregnant, they also wanted to eliminate the possibility of rape or any sexual indiscretion with a slave. For this reason, those who served the queen were those who would not be tempted by sexual interest in her.

The implication of this historical fact is that this person to whom God sent Philip was not a castrated eunuch but was probably gay since he served the Queen. Furthermore, when the Bible speaks of people being from Ethiopia, the implication is that they are African people of color.

So, what we have here is a story about how God took Philip away from a situation where he was reaching hundreds of people and sent him to a solitary, black, gay man. What an amazing example of God's love for people who the Church so often excludes and rejects. Many lesbian and gay people, like the eunuch, feel they are traveling on a desert road. Their souls are parched and thirsty. Many, like the Ethiopian eunuch, are all alone. They have reached successful positions. Their employer or boss or company trusts them, but still they carry their secret with intense loneliness. Many, like the eunuch, travel in style. They dress nicely, drive good cars, live in relative ease, but all of the things they thought would bring joy have left them hollow and empty. Many attend churches or secretly watch services on TV. Now and then they try to read the Bible. Like the Ethiopian, they may have even read from Isaiah but cannot find the good news in it for them.

Every single day of my life I hear the voices of millions of lesbian women and gay men in this country crying, "What hinders us from becoming Christians?" My passion to reach out to estranged people arises from a deep desire to answer those cries. "What hinders me from being baptized?" The only thing I can see that they do not have is a Philip to tell them there is nothing to hinder them.

There is one last thing I think we should note about Philip. When he found the eunuch, the eunuch was reading from the prophet Isaiah. Philip could explain to him what the passage meant.

One of the dreams for this book is that it will strengthen you to share with your brothers and sisters the good news you have discovered. I am not sure if Philip was ready when God needed him or if God used Philip when he was ready. I do know this: You do not have to be a theologian to share your faith. All you have to do is to simply say, "This is what happened to me ... "

Perhaps the next time you encounter a lesbian woman or gay man who is feeling excluded, cut off, isolated or dried up, you will know enough to read to her or him from Isaiah. You may want to use the passage Philip used, or maybe you will know enough to turn over a few pages to Isaiah 56:

> *Let no outsider who has joined themselves to the Lord say, "The Lord will exclude me." And let not the eunuch complain, "I am only a dry tree." This is what the Lord says: To the eunuch who worships me and chooses to do my will I will give you something better than sons and daughters, a memorial and a name in my own house and within my walls. I shall give you an everlasting name which can never be taken away. For my house shall be called a house of prayer for all people.*
>
> Isaiah 56:3-7

What a beautiful picture of the inclusive nature of the reign of Christ. It is an incredible promise to say that those excluded because of their sexuality will be "given a name better than sons and daughters ... an everlasting name that can never be taken away." It is an important promise to people who have had so much taken away from them, often by the Church. It is a promise you need to claim for yourself and to share with others. Ruth and Naomi, Jonathan and David, Philip, the centurion and his special servant, the Samaritans, Isaiah, and the eunuchs all have important things to say to lesbian and gay Christians. I'll bet your Sunday School teachers never told you all those stories. I hope they are stories you will never quit telling until everyone knows the truth that God's love includes them, too.

You all have reached out to me and others who were bruised and battered by church life that wasn't nourishing. It's still hard to stop playing the tapes of criticism in my head, but I just go to your website and read your devotionals and articles of faith and hope. Then I am fine to go out into the world, feeling like I can hold my head up high!

Keith Bowling
Myrtle Beach, SC

Chapter 4
The Lesbian/Gay Advantage

Millions of people have listened to a lie. Society and religious leaders have said people could not be lesbian or gay and Christian, and they have believed it. That lie has taken a terrible toll on our community. The damage done by one group with power marginalizing another group rends the fabric of a civil society, even for non-Christians and people with no faith tradition. For one group to assume they have the authority or right to declare that another cannot be children of God sets up a dynamic that leaves all minorities unsafe. Our job is simple: to call the lie what it is and to help people see a living example of the truth. We do not need to persuade others to become Christians or to believe as we do, but we must secure for them the right to do so if they choose.

In Chapters 2 and 3, we looked at what various passages of scripture say about being lesbian or gay and Christian. We saw that, although there are no scriptures that speak against people being homosexual, there are four or five verses that speak against certain homosexual acts associated with idolatry and pagan ritual. Don't forget: there are many more passages that speak against certain heterosexual acts. The Bible does not condemn same-sex love, nor does Jesus say anything negative toward lesbian and gay people in particular.

It is helpful to understand what the Bible does and does not say, but the truth is that scripture is most often used to support a belief or position that someone already has assumed. The most powerful argument we have that gay and lesbian people can be Christians is that we **are**. Evangelical Christianity is centered on the personal experience of the individual with God. We, who have had the experience of being children of God, bear in our souls the irrefutable proof that we can be lesbian or gay and Christian.

As kids, and certainly as teenagers, most of us felt that who we are was something of which we should be ashamed. The social pressure to conform begins at birth. Boy babies wear blue; girl babies wear pink. Variations that cannot be easily pigeonholed disturb the corporate and social mind. Long before we knew that we were triangular pegs trying to fit into square holes, the pressure to conform began to build.

Sometimes, we suspected the truth that being different made us special, not bad. The negative onslaught, however, was simply overwhelming. Most of us were forced to deny or hide the truth, often from our own conscious minds. That should not surprise us. There was a time when polls showed that a significant portion of African-Americans believed that their race was mentally inferior to whites. That is ridiculous, of course, but a mountain of prejudice can distort the clearest truth.

Today, we know that we should be wary of listening to the majority. After all, the majority once believed the world was flat, supported slavery, crucified Jesus and stoned Christians. Just look at some of the people that have been elected President by the majority. Although quite often wrong, public opinion has incredible power, especially when wielded against oppressed people. Shame is a weapon that does inconceivable damage. It is a weapon expertly used by those desperate to shore up their own insecurity. If they can make us appear *more* sinful, they can feel *less* sinful.

Almost all lesbian and gay people grew up feeling "queer." Long before we could identify why, the pain was already growing. Being different can be paralyzing for a child, and it holds a great deal of terror for adults. Although we may claim that it is for economic or vocational reasons, most people remain closeted because they fear what others might think. Shame has a tragically powerful hold on lesbian and gay people.

Having said all that, it may seem ridiculous to say that I want us to think about the advantages we have as lesbian or gay Christians. However, we do have some unique benefits that others may miss. It is easy to identify more than we could hope to address in this chapter. I'll leave the obvious ones for you to contemplate, but there are three important blessings that we must not overlook.

Sexuality

The first thing that comes to mind for most people when they think about the lesbian and gay community is sex. Actually, if we had sex as often as some people think, we'd be an exhausted, dehydrated bunch. I think much of the homophobia of the religious conservatives is a secret fear that we are having more "fun" than they are. In the minds of many religious folks, sex, or sexuality, is a shameful subject. They seem to think it is a dirty secret. If they do it with the lights off and don't talk about it then maybe God won't know. To integrate sexuality as a gift from God and an expression of our spirituality is beyond their imagining.

There is no doubt that this shameful thinking has infected lesbian and gay people too, but at least we are more open to changing that. Because our sexuality is different from the majority, most of us were forced to talk to God about it from the time we were children. Perhaps that has opened a door for us that remains hermetically sealed for most heterosexual Christians.

From the beginning of the book of Genesis, the message is that sexuality is one of God's gifts. In his book *Between Two Gardens*, James Nelson talks about integrating "eros" and "agape." Lesbian and gay Christians have a much greater chance of integrating the sanctity of both physical and spiritual love as gifts from God. The door is only open a crack, even for us, but it is an invitation to attain wholeness in a way heterosexual Christians might never know.

As Christians, we must begin to show our community how to bring God into our sexual lives. To rave or rage about sexual ethics or immorality solves little and probably makes matters worse. Most people already have more than enough shame. What we need is to be encouraged to invite God into our sexual lives and to find sexual healing. At least that is a possibility for people who are open to talking to God about their sexuality. It is an advantage that we have. If we can invite God into our bedroom, we also stand a significantly better chance of integrating our faith into other areas of our lives.

Most Christians pray before meals. We give thanks and ask God to use the food to give our bodies strength and health. Why would it be so unthinkable to ask God to bless our experience and expression of sexual intimacy? Too often we act as if it is our secret from God or a necessary evil. What a revolutionary thing it might be for us to find new ways to celebrate sexuality as one of God's wonderful gifts.

As openly lesbian and gay people, we have been honest about the biggest secret in our lives, therefore we have an opportunity to have a relationship with God that is authentic and dynamic. Our relationships need not be based upon pretense or duplicity. If we can invite God into the most intimate area of our lives, we have a better chance of more fully integrating the faith we profess.

One of the unfortunate realities about society's understanding of what it means to be lesbian or gay is that they frame it entirely in sexual terms. Referring to us as homoSEXuals renders the balance of who we are meaningless. There is so much more than just sexual attraction that makes us lesbian or gay. I have a friend who is a Roman Catholic priest who has chosen celibacy as his lifestyle. Although he has never had sex with a man *or* a woman, he still identifies himself as openly gay. Our identity extends far beyond the bounds of sexual activity.

In his wonderful book *The Soul Beneath the Skin: The Unseen Hearts and Habits of Gay Men*, David Nimmons explores many of the gifts that come with being gay and, in his exploration, gay men. He quotes long-time activist Harry Hay, the founder of the Mattachine Society, who said, "Some people say we're just the same as straight people except for what we do in bed. I say, what we do in bed is the only place where we're the same."

Sensuality

The second advantage lesbian and gay people have is the gift of sensuality. Lesbian and gay Christians seem much more attuned to the sensual gifts of life. In disproportionate numbers we are chefs, artists, musicians, designers, decorators, hairdressers, florists, healers and caregivers.

At the very center of the Christian faith is the truth that the "word became flesh." That is to say, we cannot have a healthy and coherent theology unless our starting point is the incarnation. God came to us in a physical way through the flesh of Jesus from Nazareth. Jesus was born of Mary's physical pain and nursed at Mary's breast. He dirtied his diapers, and, when he was eight days old, his penis was circumcised. Thinking of our Savior in specific physical terms may make us uncomfortable, but Jesus accomplished our redemption through his physical suffering and death.

Sloshing about in our bodies are roughly the same chemicals that are found in the ocean. The bones of our body are made out of the same basic carbon that forms rocks on the highest mountains. Our bloodstream runs with the same basic sugar compound flowing in the sap of trees. The nitrogen in our bones also makes up the soil and is a source of nutrition for the plants of the earth. We are a part of the whole of God's creation, and, from the beginning, God said that it was good, very good.

Our physical sensations are gifts from God. Sensuality was an original gift of God. In the creation parable, one result of human disobedience was that Adam and Eve became ashamed of their bodies. This was not God's original intention. God designed us in a way that our bodies give us pleasure. God put us together so that the smell of baking bread has the power to make us feel good all over. The taste of well-prepared food can make a mediocre day special. A beautiful sight makes us feel fully alive. God put us together so that sex feels good and satisfies a whole range of physical, emotional and, I believe, spiritual needs.

Have you ever read the sensual words in the Song of Solomon? It is a song of physical love and sensual passion:

> *His arms are rounded gold, set with jewels. His body is ivory work, encrusted with sapphires. His legs are alabaster columns, set upon bases of gold.*
> Song of Solomon 5:14-15a

> *Your two breasts are like two fawns, twins of a gazelle. Your neck is like an ivory tower. Your eyes are pools in Heshbon, by the gate of Bath-rabbim.*
> Song of Solomon 7:3-4a

There is no hint of physical shame in these scriptures. Life is, as it should be, sensually sweet.

Lesbian and gay Christians may be more sensitive and open to life's sensual gifts, and that is good because they are gifts from God. Our community expresses the sensual gifts of life in a wide variety of ways. We must help our community recognize God as the source of life's goodness.

Balance

Society has often ridiculed us because we are different. Within our own community, we joke about lesbians being "butch" and gay men being "sissies." I am glad we do not take ourselves too seriously. We would be a sad group if we could not laugh at ourselves. Like African-Americans and other minorities, we have co-opted much of that derision and have made it a part of our family humor, thus the sting is lessened. It is a stereotype to say that lesbians are more masculine than heterosexual women and that gay men are less masculine than straight men. It is true, however, that more women in my congregation own trucks than the women in the average Baptist church, and, I suspect, a lot more men at the Cathedral of Hope know how to sew and cook than the men at First Presbyterian. It is a great advantage we have over heterosexual Christians. We are much less locked into traditional roles. Lesbians are generally more aware of, and willing to express, the masculine side of their nature. Gay men are much more in touch with their feminine side and tend to express it more freely than heterosexual men. Psychologists recognize that every human being is a mixture of masculinity and femininity. The gift is the ability to own both sides and to honor them as gifts of God.

Again, Genesis has an important truth for us. "So God created humankind in God's image," it says, "in the image of God they were created; male and female God created them." (Genesis 1:27) We often miss, or misinterpret, an important point in this passage. Both masculinity and femininity are an integral part of the image of God. We have traditionally understood it to mean that God created both men and women. It might be equally accurate to understand that God created every woman and every man so that, like God, we embody both masculinity and femininity.

Although we have a long way to go, our community has made significant progress in renouncing the misogyny that has too long poisoned the human race. The word misogyny refers to our society's subconscious hatred of women. It manifests itself in a number of insidious ways. Everyone pays a devastating price for the oppression of the feminine in us all. I hope that we in the lesbian and gay community have begun honoring the feminine in our lives.

Honoring the feminine has expressed itself at the Cathedral of Hope in our being more open to the feminine side of God. Most of us grew up knowing, or at least knowing about, God as our heavenly Father. Now we must also work hard to know God as our heavenly Mother; otherwise, we are left with a distorted image of God.

Being in touch with both sides of oneself is a great advantage for someone seeking to become everything God created them to be. Knowing both sides of God is a blessing and a benefit for those of us seeking to embody all of the Spirit of God. The lesbian and gay Christian community has a unique opportunity to know the fullness of God.

In that famous conversation that Jesus had with Nicodemus in John 3, Jesus told Nicodemus that he had to be "born again." Another translation is "you must be born from above." It is amazing that evangelical Christianity can so emphasize the need to be born again but neglect completely that giving birth is a feminine act. Our mothers gave us birth the first time, and our Heavenly Mother is the one who gives us a new spiritual birth. Knowing this, we can own and honor both halves of our personhood because both are the image and likeness of God.

The sexism of our society penalizes three-quarters of the human race. That is, it punishes every woman and the feminine half of every man. The lesbian and gay community has a great stake in combating sexism, since it is the root of homophobia, as well as many other evils in our society. It is a root cause of our society's high rate of violence, child abuse and neglect, much of our racism, our destruction of the environment, and our unwillingness to care for the elderly, the sick, the homeless and the hungry. We have created a monster that may destroy the human race simply because we continue to value and function primarily out of our masculine side. Deification of the masculine without balance has extracted a high price from us all.

I don't want you to believe that I am putting down the masculine. As a gay man, I appreciate the masculine, but I also know that anything one-sided or out of balance becomes unhealthy and detrimental. Our society has, in thousands of ways, said that it values men more than women, the masculine more than the feminine. The result has been frighteningly destructive:

- Our masculine side sent us exploring and challenging new frontiers, but, without our feminine side, that attitude of quest and conquer has led to the exploitation of the environment, until it has endangered all life.
- Our masculine side gave us the aggression needed to take on challenges that seemed invincible, like disease and outer space, but, without our feminine side, we treated one another like enemies. War, rape, gay-bashing and murder have become a way of life.
- Our masculine obsession to obtain and to acquire has elevated our standard of living beyond what our forebears could have imagined, but, without our feminine side, we deludingly think that 6 percent of

the world's inhabitants consuming 50 percent of the world's goods is perfectly reasonable.

The list could go on, but I would hope that each of us will wonder how we might better balance the masculine and feminine in our own lives and in our world. This is a topic the lesbian and gay community must address first. We have an incredible responsibility for this matter. If we are not successful in confronting this problem, we can expect neither the Baptists nor Methodists, Catholics nor Mormons to give us leadership. Furthermore, this is a challenge that the Church itself must face because it is, at its heart, a spiritual issue.

The sexism that is so deeply rooted in our culture is almost invincible because it is rooted in our concept of God. If we only understand God in Anglo-male terms, we will honor the Anglo and masculine in humans. Failing to understand God's feminine side, we will never empower the feminine divinity that lies dormant in each of us. Until we really experience the God who is male and female, mother as well as father, we will continue to be out of balance and spin destructively out of control.

When I was in the third grade, I had a friend named Tommy. He lived near me, so we were friends before we even started school. We were in the same class in the first and second grades. One day after school, while Tommy and I waited for the bus, three kids started picking on us. At first they were just picking on Tommy because they were in his class, but when they realized that I was with him, they picked on me, too.

Something of a fight broke out, though they were the ones doing most of the fighting. Teachers came over and broke things up pretty quickly, and Tommy and I ran to catch our bus. When I sat next to him, I noticed that he was crying. I asked him if he was hurt, and he said no, he was just afraid.

I held Tommy's hand as we rode the five miles home. He got off the bus first, and I told him I'd call him later. Afterward, I realized that I was shaking. I did not understand it at the time. I was not really so afraid of those three boys; they were not any bigger than I was. I was, however, scared by the names they called Tommy and me.

I got off the bus that day and ran into the house to find my mother, but she was not home. She had taken my younger brother to the dentist. I was aware of a deep loneliness, and I went to my room and cried. I really had hoped my mother would be there because I knew that she would have held me and told me she loved me and that I was perfectly okay just as I was. She was not home, and I was alone.

As I think back, I know I really was not alone, but then no one had ever told me that I had a Heavenly Mother who would have held me and told me she loved me and that I was perfectly okay just as I was. Now I know, and that knowledge is a liberating advantage over those who know God only as Father. Knowing that both halves of my life are created in the image and likeness of God is a great asset.

The gay and lesbian community has a number of benefits beyond the three we have discussed. Perhaps these advantages have enabled us to survive relatively intact despite incredible persecution. They have given us an internal strength that we might otherwise lack. We must use that strength to be the teachers, healers and caregivers of the human race. In doing that, we will be the disciples of Jesus who came to heal, teach and care. Perhaps the lesbian and gay community is an advantage God has over evil.

I was born in 1950 and grew up when America was changing. Leaders emerged as champions of non-violent efforts to get equality in education, jobs and politics. I watched in horror at the reaction in the South to this movement and as it was met with resistance. I found comfort in church and with my family. My father was a deacon and my mother was a deaconess. Ironically, in the 1970s, I used to hear them whispering about "that place on Ross Ave." This piqued my curiosity, and, occasionally, I would sneak away and stare at the building which had become the Metropolitan Community Church of Dallas. I was caught one Sunday and was told do not ever go up there again. When my parents spoke to me in a certain tone I knew I had better listen and obey. I never went back, but it did not leave my thoughts.

Then I met her and she captured my heart. She was Catholic. I would go to church with her but felt like I was in a place that I should not have been. We eventually became members of MCC and our life together got better and better. We joined the choir, taught Sunday school and volunteered in other ministries. I felt a call to become more intimately involved, and started helping in the church office and joined the lay ministers of worship. This was very fulfilling for me and my faith grew strong. I really felt the strong presence of Jesus in my life. I owe it all to God and a gay church. I am thankful to God for his presence in our church. I truly believe that we as a gay church with outreach to all people will help facilitate changing the minds of those who seek to try to turn people against us. God is with is in all aspects of our worship. With his wisdom and guidance we will succeed.

Cece Shelmon
Dallas, TX

Chapter 5

The Homosexuality of God

Let me begin with a word of warning about this chapter. This book has been written so that lesbian and gay people might be helped and healed in their relationships with God. A secondary purpose was that this would be a book that our parents and friends might read. With that in mind, most of the material has been carefully crafted so that even those still uncertain might be invited to continue reading and consider another perspective.

I have always felt that someone who challenges my thinking is more valuable to me than someone who merely confirms what I already believe. Some of the best gifts God ever sent into my life have been people with whom I strenuously, and sometimes regularly, disagreed. Having said that, let me add that this is not how everyone responds to challenging material. This is meant to be a challenging chapter. Those who have considered these matters from this perspective before will read this and wonder what on earth I mean. Yet, if you have never thought about God from this angle, it may at least startle you.

My purpose is not to convince anyone of anything. Actually, all I hope to do is paint a picture and invite you to look at it. You may or may not like it, but hopefully it will be, at the very least, something new to see. If you find any of this offensive, please forgive me. Please also consider why it is you have reacted thus and what is so offensive about the idea that Jesus was gay.

A wise person once noted that the history of

humankind's religion can be summarized in one sentence: "In the beginning God created us in the image and likeness of God, and ever since we've been trying to return the favor." It is true that many belief systems do little more than recreate God in the image of the believer. While that is easy enough to see in other faiths, we must admit that our Judeo-Christian faith has done that as well.

It is almost impossible for any of us to conceive the One who is unlike all of creation without drawing on the creation that we know. However, women and people of color can certainly testify to the devastating results of what happens when God becomes a white man. The lesbian and gay community can also easily point out how the Religious Right has projected its own prejudices onto God. I have no doubt that when Pat Robertson closes his eyes to pray, he prays to a god that looks amazingly like himself, his father and his grandfather. The radical Religious Right worships a god who consistently thinks in right-wing, upper-middle-class, white, male, American terms.

John Wesley, the founder of Methodism, was adamant about the fact that God has given us all free will. He hated theological systems that taught that God had predetermined that some people would go to heaven and others to hell. Wesley once said he believed that the God of the predestinationist was worse than the Devil "himself." That is probably how many of us feel about the god of Pat Robertson, Jerry Falwell, James Dobson or Phyllis Schlafly. Their god is not someone we'd want to meet on a dark, lonely night, and, in my opinion, their god bears very little resemblance to the God revealed by Jesus Christ in the gospels.

Our challenge, then, is to avoid doing the exact same thing with our vision of God. I have no doubt that the God to whom I pray—the God of lesbians, gays, liberals and liberationists—is the star of many a fundamentalist's nightmare. How do we keep from creating a God who thinks like us, acts like us and looks like us? Is that even possible, since humans find it difficult to hold absolute abstract thoughts for long?

Some may argue that oppressed people need to identify with a God who clearly identifies with them. In saying, "What you do to the least you do to me" (Matthew 25:40), Jesus turned the image of God on its head. It was a statement of absolute identification with those who were without access. The difference between the need of the oppressed to worship a God who identifies with them and the Right's white, male, American God is the level of power from which we image our God.

What I mean is, the God to whom I relate as a gay person is very different from the God I might relate to as a white man. Let me admit that as a white, American male, I am a member of a privileged class. (I have to say that in the politically correct circles where I live much of my life, it doesn't feel much like a privilege most days.) Although I have many advantages of birth, I am keenly aware that an American, white, male God is very different from the God of a homosexual. Although our opponents on the right will no doubt misconstrue this statement, I must confess that I pray to a God who created, loves and embraces me as a gay person, not the god of my race, gender or nationality. It was never a conscious choice, but, over the years, I have discovered that I am much more comfortable with, devoted to and awed by the God who created me as a gay man.

These days, it is quite common to see Christ depicted as a black man in works of art. Since Jesus was born in northern Africa, that portrayal is much more accurate than the blond-haired, blue-eyed, fair-skinned Christ we often see. Nonetheless, when the black Christ first began to appear, a significant number of African-Americans were disturbed by the images and expressed their displeasure. Why?

Although I would never presume to speak for people of color, some things are common to us all. First, we are uncomfortable with images of God that differ from the images of our childhood. A black Christ didn't fit the image with which many black people had grown comfortable. It is difficult to surrender the God of our childhood, even when we outgrow it.

A broadcast of a fundamentalist church's worship service once showed the pastor making outlandish and unsubstantiated statements about a number of theological and sociological issues. As the camera panned the audience, I saw the CEO of one of the largest corporations in America. I could not imagine how a person who was that capable and brilliant could submit himself to a ministry so primitive. This example is one more reminder of the power of the gods with which we have grown comfortable.

Perhaps a more important reason some African-Americans were initially uncomfortable with a black Jesus was the notion that a black Christ didn't represent the power in the culture in which they lived. In a racist culture where whites dominate, a black Jesus lacked the power to meet needs or answer prayers. Perhaps, like African-Americans, we all long for a Savior who is more powerful than we are.

This bit of history is a sad testimony to the insidious power of racism in America. Perhaps even more frightening is the fact that this also speaks of the powerful and terrifying ways we create our societal gods in the image of those who are in power.

We still flinch, or at least notice, when someone refers to God as "she." Why is that? Why do people still object to inclusive language that uses balanced images of God? Why do we find it so hard to break ourselves of exclusively using masculine pronouns for God? The Bible is full of feminine images of God, but we have lived most of our lives without even noticing.

Our church strongly believes that being lesbian or gay is a gift, that it is something of which we should be proud. We teach and preach that lesbian and gay people are created in the image and likeness of God. Having said that, it was interesting to watch people wince a bit or snicker the first time I announced that I was going to teach on the topic of the "homosexuality" of God.

Why should that idea make us so uncomfortable? If we believe there is "nothing sinful" about being lesbian or gay, why should the idea of God being homosexual bother us? Although we don't want to be guilty of recreating God in our image, neither do we want to allow our own internalized homophobia to "heterosexualize" God. What is wrong with a God who has lesbian tendencies? Shouldn't there be at least a one-in-ten chance that God is gay? Although I say that jokingly, the idea itself challenges some of us to think about God in a whole new way.

The truth is that we are uncomfortable thinking about God in any sexual terms. It is true that there is a great danger in anthropomorphizing God. God is not human and, therefore, neither heterosexual nor homosexual. However, as Christians, we believe that God did become human in Jesus of Nazareth. We believe that Jesus is the most perfect human expression of who God is. Or as Saint Paul put it, "In Jesus dwelled the fullness of the Godhead bodily." (Colossians 2:9)

The Bible says that "Jesus was tempted in every point, like as we are." (Hebrews 4:15) If Jesus didn't struggle with attractions to men, then he was not tempted as I am. And if he didn't struggle with homosexual feelings, then how can he be the Savior of homosexual people? Of course, that does not mean that Jesus struggled with what the fundamentalists would call the "sin of homosexuality." It means that Jesus struggled, as every human does, with how to live out his sexuality in a way that is healthy, responsible and life-giving.

I deliberately decided to deal with the "sex" portion of the homosexuality of God first. There are two reasons for that. First, it is the part of the idea that is most likely to disturb us, and something that troubles us is probably something we should examine. Those things that disturb us are most often our best teachers. Although, we "enjoy" books, sermons and lectures that confirm what we already believe, we seldom grow as a result of that experience.

A major portion of our resistance to thinking about Jesus in sexual terms is rooted in our unwillingness to allow God into our sex life. It is an expression of very ancient heresies.

When I was in high school, our church youth group had this wonderful counselor. He was very devout and totally irreverent. One day, he said to us, "If you ever doubt that Jesus understands your pain, just remember that, when he was eight days old, he was circumcised with a stone knife."

That has stuck with me for a long time. Unfortunately, it got him fired as youth director—which is my point. As Christians, we must reclaim sexuality from the unbelievers. It is a gift from God to be celebrated and enjoyed. Much of our society's unhealthy, abusive and irresponsible sexual behavior comes from the refusal of the Church to deal honestly and directly with sex. Our inability to think of Jesus in sexual terms is one symptom of that denial.

We rationalize it by saying that we "reverence" Jesus too much to sexualize him. While that might sound pious, what it actually says is that we think sex is too dirty for God. As long as we treat sex as something profane and removed from God, then Jesus will never be able to redeem the sexual aspect of our lives.

Biblical, orthodox, Christian theology requires us to believe that Jesus had homosexual feelings and urges just as a significant portion of the human population does. Still, to suggest that Jesus was exclusively gay would be a distortion, because Jesus also had heterosexual feelings and urges just as a significant portion of the human population does.

The second reason I began with the "sex" in homosexuality was to get it out of the way so we can look at the fact that there is more to homosexuality than just sex.

We have talked elsewhere about the dual nature of God. God is both male and female, and so is each of us. Lesbian and gay people tend to be much more aware of their dual nature, and, as a result, in that area at least, we may be more like God.

The Bible often depicts God in "transgender" roles. Jesus referred to himself as a "mother hen." There are a wide range of both masculine and feminine images of God, and they are quite often mixed in the same verse.

For example, I once preached on the scripture from Deuteronomy where God is pictured as being like a mother eagle. The pronoun used throughout that passage is "he," but the activity that is described is something only a mother would do. You see, the female eagle is larger and considerably stronger than the male, which is why she is the one to teach the young to fly. She is more capable of catching the babies and carrying them on her wings.

In this passage, we have a classic picture of the "transgender" behavior of God. Although it can be understood as simply the product of the author's sexism, it may also be a part of a larger picture that the Bible paints of God.

Unlike the surrounding pagan religions, Judaism did not have a God and a secondary goddess. Instead, Yahweh was both and neither and all in all.

Perhaps homosexuals are uniquely connected with God because we have been forced to live with ambiguity. As humans, we have a great need for structure and control.

Most of us have learned by now that our sexual orientation is not something we have been able to control in the sense that we could change or hide it. It is a part of us that is beyond our control. It leaves us vulnerable and makes life much more ambiguous.

The "rules" of the heterosexual majority don't always apply to us. The myths, stories, guidelines and dreams that give life its structure and meaning are absent, or at least weakened, for lesbian and gay people.

Although lesbians and gays have escaped some of the oppression of other minorities because we have been able to "pass" as one of the majority, we have suffered an oppression no other minority has experienced. This oppression should have destroyed us, but it has revealed in us an amazing and incredible strength and power because we have survived.

Sociologists say that a people cannot survive more than a generation without a "story." A person who cannot remember any further back than his or her own birth is an orphan. Lesbian and gay people have been orphans from one generation to the next. For centuries, we have had to reinvent and recreate ourselves because our story has never been recorded for those who would come after us. We have left hints, small bits of threads, throughout history, and those threads have been treasured. Can you remember the first book or story or movie you experienced in which lesbian/gay love was even hinted? Do you remember the first lesbian or gay person you talked to?

Those were life-changing moments for many of us. After many years of living in an almost exclusively heterosexual world, we suddenly felt connected with "our people." Anthropologist Dr. Laurens Van Der Post, the principal chronicler of the Stone Age Kalahari bush people, explains it this way:

The supreme expression of their spirit is in their stories. They are wonderful story tellers. Their story is their most precious possession. These people know what we do not, that without a story you are not a people, or a nation, or a culture. Without a story you haven't got a life of your own.

Nobel Prize winning author Elie Wiesel, in his book *The Gates of the Forest*, tells an enchanting story of how, from one generation to the next, the teachers and leaders forget more and more of the redeeming ritual, until, finally, all they can do is recite the story of past redemptions. Wiesel, who himself survived the Nazi holocaust, concluded that telling the story was enough since "God made humans because God loves stories."

Our stories connect us to one another, to those who have gone before us, and, in a very powerful way, to God. That is why, as lesbian and gay people, we must see ourselves in the sacred stories of our faith. "Are we really there?" some would ask. The answer I can offer, without fear of contradiction, is that there is a great deal more evidence that lesbian and gay people are present in the sacred stories than there is evidence that "Americans" are present.

The Jews have survived horrifying oppression over the centuries in part because, since the time of the Exodus, one generation has recounted their stories and history to the next. There is a great story about the Baal Shem Tov, the 18th century Hasidic mystic:

One day, the Baal Shem Tov called all of his disciples around him and gave each of them an assignment. The last was Reb Yakhev, who was told that he was to travel all over Europe telling the stories of all that he had seen while he had been a disciple.

Hoping for a more prestigious assignment than

wandering storyteller, Reb Yakhev was a little disappointed. The Master, however, added that one day Reb Yakhev would tell one particular story that would be his life's crowning achievement.

And so it was that, after years of wandering and telling stories, Reb Yakhev heard of a nobleman who was paying gold to anyone who could tell him a story about the Baal Shem Tov.

Reb Yakhev thought, "This is my chance. I know a thousand stories; I'll be rich." He was warmly welcomed into the nobleman's home, but, as the time for the storytelling arrived, Reb Yakhev realized, to his horror, that he could not recall a single story. The nobleman was very gracious and suggested that Reb Yakhev rest so that he might be able to remember the stories. But the next day it was the same. On the third day, when Reb Yakhev still could not remember his stories, in humiliation, he decided to leave. The nobleman, though, was still very hospitable and encouraged him to stay.

Reb Yakhev declined but said, "There is one small story that I remember that has no meaning, but at least it will prove that I knew the great master." This was the story he told the nobleman:

Once, during the Passover, the Baal Shem Tov and I decided to take a trip to a city in Turkey. When we arrived, the city was decorated for the Christian festival of Easter. We passed safely through the town to the part of the city where the Jews were made to live. Of course, all of the doors and windows were closed and locked, since this was one of the times when Christians persecuted the Jews.

When we arrived at one particular house and knocked on the door, the people inside quickly pulled us inside. We were scolded for being about on a day like this. Didn't we know it was dangerous? The Baal Shem Tov horrified everyone by throwing back the curtains and opening the shutters. Then he stood in the window that opened right onto the town square.

There, in the square, the festival was about to begin, which meant that the people had erected a wooden cross and stacked faggots beneath it. They were about to burn the archetypal Jew, who they believed was guilty of crucifying Jesus.

As the procession began, the Baal Shem Tov noticed the Bishop leading the way dressed in his fine robes and diamonds. The master turned to me and instructed me to fetch the Bishop. I knew this would mean certain death, but it was my place to obey, not to question. So, I did as I was told. I was shocked when the Bishop heard the message and meekly followed me into the house. The Bishop and the Baal Shem Tov met for a long time. Finally, the Bishop emerged, and, after he was gone, we too returned home.

Reb Yakhev continued, meekly, "You see. I told you it was not much of a story, but at least now I hope you know that I was a disciple of the great Master." As he looked up, Reb Yakhev noticed that the nobleman was weeping uncontrollably. He did not understand until, at last, the nobleman explained. "I was that Bishop," he said. "Although I was Jewish and was descended from a long line of rabbis, it had become very disadvantageous to be Jewish in that day. During a time of great persecution, I converted to Christianity. Eventually the people even made me their Bishop. I went along with everything, even the killing of the Jew each year.

"Then, that day, when you came and told me that the Baal Shem Tov wanted to see me, I knew my shame had caught up with me at last. For three hours we talked. Finally, he told me that he thought there might still be hope for my soul if I resigned my position and spent the rest of my life helping others. His last words to me were these, 'When someone comes to you telling you your own story you will know your sins are forgiven.'

"Three days ago when you arrived, I recognized you immediately. Then, when you could remember no stories, I thought all hope was lost. Finally, you remembered one story, my story, and I know that God has forgiven me."

So it is with all of us. Nothing has the power to liberate us into communion with God like hearing someone tell our own story. Too often, lesbian and gay people have been shut out of the story of God's people. The result has been disastrous on many levels, and we have felt deprived of our connection with God.

There is a powerful sense in which that is how it is with God as well. Humanity was created out of God's longing for a connection. Because God did not have a family, God had to create a community of creatures that were, at least, somewhat like God. Humans were created in the image and likeness of God.

Our dual nature is one manifestation of that, and our free will is another. In order for genuine community to occur, God knew it would have to be something we chose, not something that was forced or compelled. So God created us as creatures that had to be left free to make right, wrong, good and bad choices.

The only way we would truly be free to choose community with God was for God to create us and withdraw to a distance that required us to relate by faith. Any more direct contact would force a relationship upon us.

God longs for an experience of family and community that has never been available. Perhaps lesbian and gay people sense that about God in our hearts. Goodness knows, we've had enough opportunity and motivation to walk away. Actually, so many have sought to drive us away that I have to wonder if they sense a spiritual connection that they do not have. It isn't that they cannot have it. You see, I don't think God discriminates on the basis of sexual orientation.

I have visited Cathedral of Hope four times since my son moved to Fort Worth from New York City, and, each and every time, I ended up crying in the middle of the service. The first couple of times I thought maybe I was just losing it, but then I realized the reason I got so emotional is because, for the first time in my life, I was feeling "true" love from the members of the Church. Every single person who attends your services is there because of their belief in God and their desire to worship him in peace and harmony.

At CoH, the minute you walk in the door, you can feel the presence of God and, most importantly, the presence of love from other members. It's a feeling so powerful the tears just overflow in me, like a cleansing of the soul. Your fellowship exemplifies the truest form of God's love (love of all people, not just a select few). I find myself watching as each beautiful soul takes communion, and I say a prayer for each of them that God will keep them safe from the bigots in the world and bring them peace within themselves.

As my son will tell you, I have many, many, adopted sons and daughters. Every gay or lesbian friend he introduces me to instantly becomes my child and I become their protector. God help the person who hurts any of my children in any way. Matt is my only blood-related child, but my other children are just as precious to me. And, for the record, I wouldn't trade my gay son for all the straight children in the world. God gave him to me for a reason, and I intend to love him unconditionally and protect him as best as I can for as long as I'm allowed. God bless you and all in your church for all that you do for the spirits of these wonderful, blessed children. I look forward to my next visit to your church.

Patricia Scott
Waco, Texas

Chapter 6
Homophobia can be Cured!

Senator McCarthy had his "Red Scare." George Wallace had his "Negro Problem." Ronald Reagan had his "Evil Empire." Now, Pat Robertson, James Dobson and the Religious Right have found a convenient target in the lesbian and gay community. By filling the airwaves and fundraising letters with images of "radical homosexuals," they have succeeded in finding a socially acceptable scapegoat for their fear-based fundraising. Some have suggested that using the "threat" of gay marriage got George W. Bush elected to a second term as President.

Most people are not so conspicuous in their divisive political-theology, but then few people are as motivated to raise millions of dollars to fund religious empires or political dynasties. Lesbian and gay people have often been innocent pawns in fundraising tactics. The Religious Right has a concrete and material need to foster continued homophobia in our society by portraying lesbian and gay people as evil threats to the family and to the American way of life. It seems irrelevant to this group that it maliciously distorts characterizations of homosexuals. It seems to be of little concern that it has done incomprehensible harm to the well-being of hundreds of thousands of lesbian and gay people and their families.

By creating a homophobic atmosphere in this country, the Religious Right has fostered a period of violence and abuse against the lesbian and gay community. To have done so against any other minority would have resulted in the hate-mongers being ostracized by civilized society. Were these zealots to stereotype African-Americans in such distorted terms, the Anglo churches of this country would rise up and denounce them. Were the extremists to use prejudice against Latin-Americans to fill their coffers, the morally just would banish and scorn them. Again, we must ask people of good conscience why it is that lesbian and gay citizens are fair game for such victimization.

An African-American heterosexual friend called the lesbian and gay community "the niggers of the Nineties." With language that makes me squirm, she goes on to explain that, in our day, the most visible and vocal leaders of the Church use their spiritual framework to create division and distrust. If one could return to the 1960s and read the writings and sermons of the spiritual leaders of that day (like W.A. Criswell, longtime pastor of one of the nation's largest Southern Baptist churches, First Baptist in Dallas), it would be easy to recognize a repeating pattern. Sunday morning from 11-noon is still the most racially segregated hour in America, but it is considered unethical, even sinful, to be racist today.

We must beware that 30 years from now, as with racism, all we will have accomplished with homophobia is to make it more subtle and insidious. The most devastating aspect of homophobia is how easily it is internalized. Although the homo-hatred that the Religious Right tries to stir up can cost us our jobs, our children and even our lives, it is when we let that poison seep into our own living that our souls are most endangered.

Internalized homophobia is toxic to our hopes, dreams, relationships and health. Rev. Troy D. Perry, founder of the Universal Fellowship of Metropolitan Community Churches, calls it "oppression sickness." That is an accurate depiction of what often happens to members of our community when we allow the homophobia of our society to infect our souls. It is, at times, like a virus that ravages our lives; in other ways, it can be like a low-grade fever.

Although there are many ways in which internalized homophobia manifests itself and works its evil, none is more damaging than the one we call "the closet." It should be obvious that a person who has to live a life in hiding has a severely limited chance to become the happy, healthy, holy person God intended. Like a flower longing to express itself in all of its beauty, so it is that every human life needs to express the truth about the beautiful person God created. A human life can no more bloom in the lightless atmosphere of a closet than a rose could bloom in the dark.

I know that options are limited for many of us who have sensitive jobs, but it is important that we acknowledge that the cost of living in a closet commonly exceeds the value of almost any job. If we live our lives so that shame or bigotry controls us, our lifestyle will inevitably begin to manifest unhealthy and self-destructive behaviors.

I never saw Gene before the day he walked into my office. He refused to tell me his real name, and he showed up wearing sunglasses, even inside. I have very little patience with that sort of thing, but Gene seemed so desperate for help that I gave him a break. As it turned out, Gene was a graduate of an Ivy League school and a member of one of the best law firms in town. He was very active in one of the largest Presbyterian churches, where he served as a deacon. His activity in various social and cultural causes led to his name being mentioned as a possible candidate for local office.

He spent most of our time together explaining all of the reasons it was essential for him to remain deeply closeted. It did not require the gift of prophecy to foresee that Gene was on a fast track to ruin. Unfortunately, he quickly discounted the counsel I offered because I was not a "normal preacher." When he left my office, I felt very sad for this deluded man.

The next time I saw Gene was in the newspaper.

It seems that he was murdered late one night in a city park. He had gone there to meet a guy, but the one he met was not looking for the same thing Gene was. His murderer was a 20-year-old who later testified he killed Gene as a part of a ritual gang initiation. A requirement of gang membership was to find and "beat a queer severely enough that he required hospitalization." The man who killed Gene started beating him and did not stop until almost every bone in his body was broken.

A Dallas, Texas, judge thought the killer deserved a lighter sentence because the victim was gay. The loneliness of Gene's closet drove him to behave in unsafe and unhealthy ways that ultimately cost him his life. He was too closeted to go to church or clubs or even bars to meet another person, but in the end the whole world knew his secret. Gene's self-violence was more obvious than most. Other lesbian and gay people allow their internalized shame to drive them to addictions, to destroy their relationships, to limit their career choices, to isolate them from their families, and even to lead them to suicide.

Bruce Hilton begins his book *Can Homophobia Be Cured?* with a letter from a mother whose son committed suicide nine years prior. She writes, "To all the Bobbys and Janes out there I say these words to you, as I would to my own precious children: 'Please don't give up hope in life or in yourself.'" She went on to attribute the suicide of her own son, Bobby, to the homophobia and ignorance of almost all Protestant and Catholic churches. She painfully and honestly confessed how she became trapped in the bondage of homophobia and came to believe that Bobby needed to repent or God would condemn him to hell:

> *Looking back, I realize how depraved it was to instill false guilt in an innocent child's conscience*

causing a distorted image of life, God, and self,
leaving little, if any, feeling of personal worth.

This mother very accurately describes the dynamics that, to some extent, take place in the heart of every lesbian or gay person growing up in a homophobic society like ours. The Rev. Paul Tucker, a colleague and former member of the Cathedral of Hope's pastoral staff, identifies five symptoms of this inner poisoning in the lives of lesbians and gays:

- **Self-loathing**. Often the abuse that is heaped upon us by society is replicated in the way we treat ourselves and one another. This is manifested in various ways. It would be fair to ask if the high rate of smokers in our community is a manifestation of this self-punishment. Another frightening demonstration is that there are still people in our community participating in unprotected sex.
- **Addictions**. This is a way to medicate inner pain. Alcohol abuse is most common, but sexual addictions, overeating and other compulsive behaviors are prevalent.
- **Fragile Relationships**. Jesus said that we were to love others as we love ourselves. He seemed to recognize that it was impossible to love another person without being able to love oneself. Internalized homophobia greatly limits our capacity to love another person. Add to that the absence of support and the inherent difficulty of maintaining long-term relationships, and it is remarkable that any lesbian or gay relationship lasts.
- **Compartmentalization**. Internalizing the bigotry of society leads to dividing our lives into disconnected compartments. In my opinion, the most harmful example of this is that most lesbian and gay people

keep their sexuality and spirituality completely separated. Integration of one's values and gifts is almost impossible when a significant portion of one's life is locked away in some isolated closet.

- **The "black hole" effect**. Scientists think that the collapse of stars forms black holes. The result of the collapse is the formation of a hole in space that seems to swallow up all of the light that comes its way. When people have internalized as much poison as we classically do, we become drained of energy, hope and joy. Depression, despondency and doubt can become a way of life.

Because AIDS has tragically outed a number of closeted men, we have a sad picture of our capacity for self-hatred. Roy Cohn was an assistant to Senator McCarthy and used sexual orientation to ruin dozens of lives. Terry Dolan helped to raise millions of dollars for right-wing political candidates and causes that worked to continue the oppression of the lesbian and gay community. A civil rights leader widely known to be a closeted gay man once attacked my church. The list goes on, and it is tempting to condemn these men as hypocrites of the worst sort. Yet, when we laugh at "fag" or "dyke" jokes, when we remain silent at the ridicule of another, or when we allow misinformation to go unchallenged, then we differ from them only in the scope of our hypocrisy. Such acts deepen our shame until we become more capable of self-destructive deeds.

Establishing the range of damage caused by homophobia compels us to ask what can be done to heal this epidemic. The healing must be both internal and external. The internalized bigotry will not subside until our social attitudes eradicate it. How can that be done?

Education

Studies have demonstrated that the more educated people are, the less homophobic they tend to be. There are exceptions to that, just as it is still possible to find racist people teaching in universities. The most effective method of education, however, does not take place in a classroom. It is education that takes place across dinner tables, on tennis courts, in offices and in car pools. In other words, if we really want to change society's attitude toward us, we are going to have to come out so people can put a face on their prejudice.

Homophobia would end tomorrow if we awakened to a phenomenon that caused every lesbian and gay person in the world to turn purple. People would be so shocked that the folks they respect, idolize and love are some of "those people." By coming out to our family, friends and coworkers, we force them to reevaluate their erroneous ideas about who and what homosexuals are.

Social Activism

Society will never "give" us our civil rights. It is unreasonable to expect that it would impart liberty to us more readily than it did to African-Americans or women. We must work hard and pay a great price if we are going to win our civil liberties.

As long as it is legal to discriminate against people purely on the basis of sexual orientation, social attitudes will resist substantial change. It is vital that we fight to provide a legal context in which discrimination based on sexual orientation is unacceptable. That will not cure homophobia, but it will provide a healthier environment for reducing the effect of the poison. Jesus said his followers were to be the "salt of the earth." Working to make this society better for all people is one of the best ways I know to fulfill that command.

Reframe the Issue

I suspect that if we are ever going to loosen the stranglehold of heterosexism, we are going to have to reframe the issue so that the larger community can begin to understand the price it pays. Frederick Douglas described what he called the "dehumanizing effects of slavery" not only on slaves, but also on white people, whose ownership of slaves corrupted their humanity. We must identify for others what prejudice costs them. What would a homophobia-free community be like?

Homophobia has destroyed the families of many lesbian and gay people. I get so angry when people say that we are "anti-family." Just where do they think we came from, the pumpkin patch? Every gay man or lesbian came from a family. Some of them were good; some of them were bad. But almost all of us have families. Warren J. Blumenfeld, in the introduction to his book *Homophobia: How We All Pay the Price*, writes:

> No matter what their constitution, families will continue to produce lesbian, gay, bisexual, and trans-gender offspring. The political right argues loudly that homosexuality poses a direct threat to the stability of the "traditional" nuclear family. In actuality, however, it is homo-phobia that strains family relationships by restricting communication among family members, loosening the very ties that bind. Children, fearing negative reactions from parents, hold back important information about their lives. Parents often not wanting to hear about their child's sexual or gender identity, never truly get to know their children. Even when parents and children reside in the same house, secret on secret adds up to polite estrangement and sometimes to a total break.

Far from being an enemy of the family, if we could help parents and children to be more open and honest about issues such as sexuality, we probably could save the family in a much healthier form.

Imagine the benefits to children of not being forced to deny or repress their feelings for fear of being called queer. Little boys could grow up substantially less violent if they did not have to prove they were not sissies. Little girls could develop skills that have heretofore been limited to boys. Children would be loved for whom they are rather than whom they ought to be, and that should be incredibly liberating in numerous other areas of their lives. All children, not just those who are lesbian or gay, need to develop without fear of being different. Imagine what gifts we might discover within the hearts and lives of our children if they were encouraged to be, uniquely, the people God created them to be.

Living in a society free of homophobia would strengthen almost all of our relationships. The heterosexual male's difficulty in sustaining intimate relationships has become a cliché. Limitations that society places on male bonding are often the root of the anxiety. For a little boy to get "too close" to another boy is considered "dangerous." Thus, at a critical developmental juncture, the child receives a clear signal to pull back. Increasingly, intimacy becomes equated with sexual relationships, and males feel compelled to compartmentalize their feelings.

Our culture customarily frames male-female relationships in sexual terms. The more basic and healthy relationships of friendship and mutual respect go almost ignored. Deep, genuine and intense friendship between heterosexual men and women is essentially unheard of today. Even when depicted in literature, film or television, it consistently has sexual overtones. How else can the man prove he is not gay except by his sexual attraction to any, and every, attractive woman?

Historically, women's relationships with one another have survived better. Perhaps that is for the same reasons that the Bible largely ignored lesbian acts. Our sexist society has treated women as unimportant and paid little attention to how women related to one another. As the role of women in our culture changes, however, we are seeing their relationships with each other beginning to deteriorate.

Can homophobia really be cured? It would be foolhardy for us to assume that any prejudice ever yields easily. Scientific facts and documentation will erode some underpinnings, but real change has little connection with the facts. My secret source of hope comes from the reality of my own experience. As a white male who grew up in South Georgia, I know first hand the strength with which bigotry can grip one's life. The culture and home in which I was reared were typically racist. Now, many years later, I am not so foolish as to claim that my life is free of racism, but I do know that I have made substantial progress in eradicating that evil from my life. If that change is possible, so too should it be possible for individuals and for our society to renounce the fear, prejudice and discrimination that constitutes homophobia.

Let me return to the letter that Bruce Hilton uses in the introduction to his book. The mother writing the letter closes with these words:

> *As a result of my son's suicide, I have joined other caring people to try to make a pathway with knowledge and understanding within our public school system, a pathway that in time may be traveled with dignity and freedom from fear, for gay and lesbian students, and for any student who is subjected to discrimination.*

It was at Cathedral of Hope where I finally was able to really accept the fact that God's love is unconditional. It is funny; when you finally accept yourself and love yourself as God loves you it becomes easier to genuinely love others and be tolerant and sensitive to them. I am learning to allow the love of God to flow through me and it is a wonderful feeling.

Rudy Guerrero
Dallas, Texas

Chapter 7
The Moral Minority

*There **are** Holy Homosexuals*

The words "homosexual" and "holy" seldom appear in the same sentence or, for that matter, in the same thought. That's unfortunate, since, I would say, many of the lesbian and gay Christians that I know are holy.

Holiness has many meanings and levels. It is a word frequently used in the Bible and used in various ways. The Bible describes God as holy to the extent that it is a principle characteristic of God and of all that belongs to God. The temple and all of the implements that had been dedicated to God were considered holy. God said to Israel, "You shall be holy for I your sovereign God am holy." (Leviticus 11:45) The first book of Peter refers to Christians as "a royal priesthood and holy people." The word "saint" means "holy one." Although we use saint to describe a spiritual "superhero," the New Testament uses it as a word for any believer. In that sense, at least, every lesbian woman or gay man who believes in Jesus Christ is a holy person, a saint.

In recent days, we have come to realize that both the word and the concept of holiness are linked to the idea of wholeness. Our holiness is linked with our wellness. That does not mean that people who are physically ill are not holy, but it does mean that the more mentally and spiritually healthy we are, the more holy we are. For us, this means that holiness comes only to the extent that we grow comfortable with integrating our spirituality and our sexuality. In this sense, we are working to become holy people.

Perhaps a more pervasive meaning for the word

implies a moral and ethical lifestyle. It is a biblical concept that those persons or things that belong to God take on the very nature of God. That is, since God is holy, God's people should be holy. We should begin to reflect the character of God. I have seen the nature of God reflected in the sacred way many lesbian and gay Christians live their lives. Unfortunately, they are not the ones filmed in the pride parades or protest marches.

It would be very easy for us to discard entirely the moral and ethical standards of our heterosexually-dominated world. That would be a mistake. It would be an equal mistake, however, for us to adopt them wholesale as if they are all healthy and life-giving.

With much trepidation, I will begin to address the issue of morality and ethics in the lesbian and gay community. I do not wish to imply that I have any expertise in this area. However, as a pastor, it is my responsibility to offer some guidance about how we are to live as Christians. If the Church doesn't offer guidelines for Christian decision-making, then who can lead us? What follows is geared for, but not limited to, readers who are Christian, considering Christianity, or are at least open to being guided by the principles of Jesus Christ.

Most Christians, whether gay or straight, are frightened by the thought that we might one day have to account for living out the faith we profess. But why should that be so startling? Isn't that what the Bible means when it speaks of a day of judgment? Accountability, responsibility, duty—our generation rarely embraces these concepts. What does the Bible teach us as lesbian and gay people about living morally and ethically responsible lives? Does it mean simply to live by heterosexual standards or none at all? What about the fact that those standards do not seem to be working for them? Is it okay for everyone to just decide for themselves what is right and wrong? Does God have nothing to say about the matter? How can we live with integrity without falling into legalism? Is holiness an outmoded concept for modern homosexuals?

In the Gospel of John, the disciples tried to engage Jesus in a discussion about why a man had been born blind:

> *As he passed by, he saw a man blind from his birth.*
> *And his disciples asked him, "Rabbi, who sinned,*
> *this man or his parents, that he was born blind?"*
> *Jesus answered, "It was not that this man sinned,*
> *or his parents, but that the works of God might*
> *be made manifest in him ..." As he said this, he*
> *spat on the ground and made clay of the spittle and*
> *anointed the man's eyes with the clay.*
>
> John 9:1-6

Jesus was clear that, in this case, the suffering was not the result of sin. The man's blindness was just something that happened, and it provided an opportunity for God to act in this man's life.

What would Jesus have said if the man was blind because his father had beaten his mother while she was pregnant? That kind of abuse is obviously a sin, isn't it? What if this man's blindness was the result of syphilis contracted from too many visits to the city's brothel? Would Jesus have given a different answer to the disciples' question?

As you can see, the discussion of ethics and morality results in many more questions than answers. Although I wish I could easily say that this was something you had to work out on your own, the truth of the matter is that helping you work it out is the job of the Church and my job as a pastor. It is not my job, nor the Church's, however, to tell you how you must live.

I approach this subject fearfully because this is where

the heterosexual churches we came from were most abusive. A brief sojourn to the religious television networks is all the proof one needs that these preachers are still using words like "sin," "evil," "transgression" and "immorality" to bash people whose shortcomings they may not share. Does their abuse of these concepts mean they are not real?

No, we still struggle against the reality of evil. We still violate God's laws in ways that we can only call sinful, and, too often, we treat one another in ways that are clearly immoral. We, as lesbian and gay Christians, must discover and establish what it means to live ethical, moral and healthy lives. But how do we live with integrity without becoming legalistic and abusive?

We should note that, according to evangelical theology, one of the reasons Jesus came in the first place was that the rules were not working. If rules had made people saints, the Pharisees of Jesus' day would have created heaven on earth. They had a detailed law for every occasion. There was a clear and explicit system of what was right and what was wrong. No one was ever left wondering.

Time and again they were infuriated because they thought Jesus was flouting their laws. Later in the ninth chapter of John, you will find that Jesus almost caused a riot because he healed the blind man on the Sabbath. The Pharisees took the Law's instruction not to work on the Sabbath very seriously, and medicine was work. Notice that Jesus did not just say a prayer; he might have gotten away with that. Jesus mixed up a potion and put it on the man's eyes. By the Pharisee's standards, what he did was clearly immoral.

With 2,000 years of crystal-clear hindsight, it is easy to see how foolish and meanspirited fundamentalists of the day were in using that law. But what happens to a system when you start making exceptions to the rules? Soon you have a world where the idea of setting one day each week aside for rest and for God is almost completely lost. You have a world where even pastors are workaholics. Soon you have a world with no time kept for God and renewal.

Yet if rigid rules do not work, by what authority do we decide what is right and what is wrong? As Christians, our standard in all things, including morality, is Jesus. Remember, fundamentalists of his day considered Jesus immoral. He noted that John the Baptist came practicing fasting and self-denial, and everyone said he was crazy. Jesus came feasting and celebrating life, and they called him a glutton and a drunkard.

I suspect that today's fundamentalists might well find Jesus' brand of morality suspect. He ate and drank with questionable women and unethical men. He traveled in the company of Samaritan outcasts and made heroes of wandering prodigals. Jesus would never get elected as the pastor of First Church, and I wonder how he would fare in my congregation. The Pharisees thought their morality exceeded Jesus', and in a sense they were right. They were much more fastidious about keeping the various little details of the Law than he was, but Jesus' brand of ethics was much tougher than theirs in another way.

You see, they had the Law. It was simple, straightforward and clear. However, Jesus called people to live lives that were healthy, compassionate and responsible. That is a much higher and more difficult lifestyle than rule-keeping. When you read the Gospels, you see that Jesus applied those three principles to everything he said and did. His whole life was an expression of health, love and accountability.

Jesus' life had integrity. Remember, the word integrity shares its roots with the word integrate. The difference between fundamentalist morality and Jesus' integrity was that Jesus integrated the principles of God into his life. The Pharisees tried to live by the rules, like the one about the

Sabbath. Jesus integrated the principle of the Sabbath into his life and let that principle guide all he did. That is why he had to remind them that the Sabbath was made for humanity, not humanity for the Sabbath. Jesus had internalized the purpose and point of this law into his life.

By integrating the principle behind the law, he could make ethical decisions, even when one law ("love your neighbor") came into conflict with another ("keep the Sabbath"). Too often we have the truth in our head but have never been able to integrate it into our lives. This is due, in large part, to the nonsensical garbage we learned as children. Another barrier to integrating healthy truths is that most of us still do not believe in our heart of hearts that we are good daughters and sons of God.

Having internalized so much shame and so many negative self-images, it is almost impossible for lesbian and gay Christians to let the light and life of Jesus shine through them. As lesbian and gay Christians, we have had to throw out much of the stuff we learned when we were kids about right and wrong. The problem is that most of us made one of two mistakes:

- We got rid of just enough of our faith to let us acknowledge our sexuality, but not enough to let us feel good about it, or ...
- We decided that if the Church was wrong about it being bad to be lesbian or gay, it must have been wrong about everything else, so we threw all of it away.

Either response is probably unhealthy.

Principles of health, compassion and responsibility must, like Jesus, guide our lives. We must ask the following questions about every action, reaction, attitude and habit:

- Is it healthy? Does this action or attitude arise from my health or from my brokenness? Does it contribute to my health or does it reinforce the brokenness of my life?
- Is it compassionate? Will this action or attitude be good for others that might be involved? Does it contribute to the health of others, or does it reinforce the brokenness of their lives?
- Is it responsible? How does God feel about it? Does it make the world a place more like the reign of God, or will my action make this an even more unhealthy and toxic place in which to live?

Increasingly, we must come to understand the link between holiness and wholeness. It is impossible to have one without the other. In an earlier chapter, I joked about a pastor who, while overweight, taunted homosexuals of being guilty of the sin that destroyed Sodom. The prophet Ezekiel quotes God as saying that one of the sins of Sodom was that they were overfed. The Bible clearly connects a healthy lifestyle and a holy lifestyle. In the second chapter of Mark, friends bring a fellow to Jesus for healing, and Jesus heals him by forgiving his sins:

> *And when Jesus saw their faith, he said to the paralytic, "My son, your sins are forgiven ... I say to you, rise, take up your pallet and go home." And he rose, and immediately took up the pallet and went out before them all.*
>
> Mark 2:5-12

Medical science is increasingly proving the correlation between the health of our soul and our physical state. Being holy is not about keeping an arbitrary set of rules, though at times it is about letting those rules keep us. Like the Sabbath laws, what God offered to us were truths to guide us to living healthy, holy, happy lives. God did not intend for the laws to be ancient programming for androids whose behavior was always and inflexibly dictated by that programming. Jesus continually got into trouble with the Pharisees because he integrated the principles into his life but disdained the crippling restrictions of legalism. The result was a life that was genuinely holy and whole.

Being a holy person does not mean being a perfect person ... or does it? One of the toughest verses in the Bible to me has always been Matthew 5:48, which says:

> Be ye therefore perfect even as your God in heaven
> is perfect.

I once allowed members of my church to select texts about which they wanted me to preach. Several people selected this one, since they had been struggling with this seemingly impossible command by Jesus. As I began to consider this teaching, which we find in the Sermon on the Mount, I consulted every translation of the Bible that I had in my office, hoping I could find one that would let me off the hook easily.

This is what I found: The King James Version, Revised Standard Version, Today's English Version, Jerusalem Bible, New International Version, J.B Philip's Bible, and even The Living Bible all said about the same thing:

> Be perfect even as your Father in heaven is perfect.

No help. After looking long and hard, I did find that the two newer translations of the Bible seemed as uncomfortable with this verse as I was. *The New Jerusalem Bible* translates the verse this way:

You must therefore set no bounds to your love, just as your God in heaven sets no bounds on how you are loved.

Well, I don't know about you, but if I could do that, I would be perfect.

One of the newer translations of the Bible, The Revised English Bible, says:

There must be no limit to your goodness, just as your heavenly parent's goodness knows no limits.

This may be even worse! The one thing I have learned is that there is no way I can be good enough for God, let alone be as good as God.

In desperation, I did what preachers always do with verses that they would like to discard. I checked the Greek translation. The problem is that the Greek word "teleios," translated "perfect," means just that! This is not a mistranslation.

This was not the first time in my life that I wrestled with this verse. During my ordination in the United Methodist Church and admission as a member at the Annual Conference, I had to answer a series of questions. The first question was, "Have you faith in Christ?" Well, that one was easy enough, but the queries did not waste any time before getting harder. The second question was, "Are you going on to perfection?" I do not know if any of the hundreds of thousands of Methodist ministers over the years ever did this, but it was tempting to say, "Yes, I'm going on to perfection just as soon as I finish telling this lie."

Actually, I wanted to say, "Yes, I'm going on to perfection, and about a thousand years after the resurrection, I should make it." I could not respond that way, though, because the third question was, "Do you expect to be made perfect in this life?" "In this life?" Whoa! How do we respond to questions like these? How do you respond to Jesus' command? What does it mean to be perfect as God is perfect? What would that look like? What would that feel like?

This is somewhat like washing an elephant—I don't know where to begin. Let's begin with what we do know. I think one thing that is clear is that God is perfect. But what does that imply? When we say God is perfect, what do we mean? Or, what don't we mean? Well, God is not a perfect flower, and God is not a perfect building, nor a perfect star. God is not a perfect man, nor a perfect woman, nor a perfect animal. God is perfect, and God is perfectly God.

Jehovah God is not perfectly Mike Piazza. I guess I should add that Mike Piazza is not perfectly God. That's okay, though. God is not supposed to be me, and I am not supposed to be God. God is the only one who should be perfectly God, and I am the only one who is supposed to be perfectly me.

Rabbi Zusia, a famous late-19th Century Hasidic scholar, once said:

> *When on that great and awesome day when I come to stand before God to give an accounting of all those things that I have done in the flesh while on this earth, God will not ask me why I was not Moses, but will ask me why I was not Zusia.*

It is true that God does not expect us to be that which God did not create us to be. That may seem obvious, but I think much of Christianity's struggle (and much of our own) has been about beating ourselves up for not being what we are not expected to be. Maybe that all sounds like a lot of double-talk, but we are not expected to be perfectly intelligent. We were all created with less than perfect intelligence, in spite of what some of us seem to think. When we do not know something, or do not know how to do something, that is not a sin on our part. For example, we are not sinful when we do not know how to communicate perfectly. We are not accountable for what we do not know. We are accountable for what we do with what we do know. We should not expect to have perfect bodies, because not one of us was created with a perfect body. Not perfectly possessing knowledge or skills or abilities does not mean that we are imperfect and have failed to live up to Jesus' command.

One of the uses of the Greek word "teleios" was to indicate that something had served its intended purpose. In fact, the word's root, "telos," means an "end," "purpose," "aim" or "goal." Could that be what Jesus is challenging us to do? Not that we achieve some level of flawlessness, rather that we discover who and what we were made to be and then become that person. That is a marvelous concept when you consider how many of us have lived out our sexuality. Here we find Jesus challenging us to come out of our closets and to be perfectly whom God created us to be.

One of my favorite stories comes out of an elementary school in Cincinnati. The whole class had to stand and tell the rest of the class something special about themselves. Little Martha Taft rose to introduce herself, and she said, "My name is Martha Bowers Taft. My great-grandfather was President of the United States. My grandfather was a United States Senator. My daddy is the U.S. Ambassador to Ireland, and I am a Brownie."

Isn't it a wonderfully freeing thing to know that God does not expect us to be anything that we are not? Yet God does expect us to be perfectly all that we are. Jesus was saying, "You shall be perfectly you, just as your God in heaven is perfectly God."

God's will for us is:

- that we be restored to the completeness for which we were created,
- that our brokenness be mended,
- that we neutralize the bitterness and anger and grief that poison our system,
- that we be as strong, as mature and as healthy as who we are allows us to be, and
- that our actions, attitudes, and values arise out of our wholeness and strength.

That is the "perfection" for which we should strive. That is what it means for us as lesbian and gay Christians to be holy and whole.

Thomas Aquinas told a story of a man who traveled all over the world in search of a special ox. He spent his life and all his fortune looking for it. At last, just moments before he died, he realized that he had been riding it all along. What a tragedy it would be if we spent our whole lives trying to be perfectly someone else. It would be a twice-wasted life, because we would miss growing into the perfect us that God created.

When Bishop William Cannon asked me those questions before ordaining me as a Methodist minister, I think he got tongue-tied. Or maybe God intervened on my behalf, because when he asked, "Are you going on to perfection?" he asked instead, "Are you **growing** on to perfection?" I could say yes to that, because I knew that to be alive is to be growing.

Several times over the years, I have quoted the feminist poster that says, "In most jobs a woman must be twice as good to be considered a man's equal; fortunately, that is not difficult." There is some truth in that, but there is even more truth in the reality that for lesbian and gay people to be considered moral, ethical or holy, we are going to have to be twice as healthy, compassionate and responsible as the society around us. Unfortunately, that is not usually tough to do either.

Lesbian and gay Christians must avoid the trap of legalism, but we also must work especially hard to ensure that we have integrated the life and teachings of Jesus into our own lives. One person who seemed to have done that well was Dag Hammarskjold. He was a superb and uncompromising man of peace and justice. During the Depression, he worked for the unemployed and homeless, though neither of these evils would have ever threatened him personally since he came from a wealthy family.

In 1953, he was elected Secretary General of the United Nations, and, in 1957, he was overwhelmingly reelected. He gained universal respect as a person of integrity and peace because his handling of the Suez Canal Crisis in 1956 may have averted World War III. My favorite prayer by him is:

For all that has been, thanks!
For all that shall be, yes!

In 1961, Secretary General Hammarskjold was on a peace mission to the Belgian Congo when he was killed in a tragic airplane crash. Following his death, the Nobel committee broke its own rules and awarded its Peace Prize to Dag Hammarskjold posthumously. No other person has been so honored. At the award ceremony, Adlai Stevenson said of him, "He was a person of faith. He was a person of compassion. He was a person of integrity." Stevenson might have also added, "He was a person who was gay."

In 1979, Jerry Falwell formed an organization called The Moral Majority. Unfortunately, the brand of morality they advocated was legalistic, abusive, demeaning and judgmental. Unfortunately, that is what the majority all too often means by being moral. What Jesus means is living healthy, compassionate and responsible lives. What our world needs today is an authentic moral minority of women and men who live out the ethics and morality of Jesus Christ. May God help us to be just such a minority.

I am a 64-year-old retired businessman in California. I am gay and have been married to a woman for 40+ years. She knows I am gay and has been extremely supportive and also is a great champion for gay causes. I was raised in the Conservative Baptist Church. I knew early on that there was something "different" about the way I felt regarding boys/men. My parents were both Sunday School teachers, and one day I asked if we could take a friend of mine with us. My father looked at me (I was in junior high school) and said, "He's queer and we don't want to take him with us and you should stay away from him." I knew then, more than ever, I would never share my feelings with my family.

When I retired and got a computer at home, somehow I came across CoH. I have sat here WEEKLY for the last couple of years. Sometimes my wife joins me, and I listen and watch attentively. Everything I thought about myself, I have come to understand is not true. I am not despised by God; I am not bound for the bowels of hell. I am a unique creation of His and loved by Him, I am not alone, I can worship here with you there at CoH. I can't describe to you the feeling of relief and love CoH has brought me. I was scared, wondering how a God who I was told loved everyone could turn his back on me once he found out I was gay. Now I know, he created me, he didn't "find out." You are doing a work there in Dallas that must please our Lord more than could ever be described. THANK YOU for your faithfulness, your love and concern for others and for preaching the truth, for getting through to me and getting me to understand that I am just fine exactly as I am. I am SO GRATEFUL to you and the work of the Cathedral of Hope!

Paul Anderson
California

Chapter 8

Come Out, Come Out, Whoever you Are

There are many levels of coming out. It is impossible to write a single chapter that anticipates exactly where each reader is on their journey. In my own life, I often think that I am about as out as anyone can get. But every now and then, I discover yet another level on which I have not fully resolved my sexual identity. In some ways, coming out is like peeling an onion. You do it one layer at a time, and you cry a lot.

Not so very long ago the term "coming out" referred to a party or celebration a young woman was given when she (and her family) came to the realization that the girl was now a woman. It was a time of excitement and celebration by family and friends. It was a time of transition and acceptance. Today, of course, coming out has taken on a completely different meaning. It usually refers to the act of a gay, lesbian or bisexual person revealing their sexual orientation to another person. As Michelanglo Signorile said in his book *Outing Yourself*, "Coming out of the closet doesn't necessarily mean telling everyone you run into that you are gay, lesbian or bisexual. What it really means is that you no longer worry about being 'discovered' by friends, family or coworkers."

Unfortunately, coming out about our sexuality is still seldom celebrated by family and friends. I believe that the day will eventually arrive when people will accept, embrace and even celebrate the acceptance by a loved one of their orientation. That day is still a ways in the future, but we can work and pray for it so that those children in daycare may have an easier time than we have had coming to grips with the truth about our lives.

A number of years ago, in a very public case, a gay man was murdered after he revealed that he had a crush on another young man. This was revealed on one of those exploitative and degrading talk shows. The young man on whom he had the crush became his murderer.

At the trial, the murderer's defense was that he had been humiliated on national television and went temporarily insane. The jury agreed to some extent and found him guilty of **second**-degree murder, even though the murder was premeditated and deliberate. The jury reasoned that being told you were loved by another man somehow made the murder less serious. What was insane about the whole affair was that no one seemed to question why this man would be **humiliated** to discover that another man liked him and was attracted to him.

The depth of homophobia revealed by this sordid case was staggering, yet not a single article, commentator or reporter mentioned that perspective on the case. Even the murdered boy's family seemed more embarrassed than grief-stricken. The average American seemed to blame the talk-show host as much as the man who pulled the trigger. No one seemed to question the underlying assumption of homophobia that created an atmosphere where murder was a response to affection.

Coming out today is still an act of great personal courage in many settings. Each person must decide to whom, and when, they reveal the intimate facts of their lives. Although many activists would argue that we must at least be willing and able to come out to everyone, that has to be an individual's decision. It is fair to say that we must all act with as much courage as possible if we are to be free, but no one has the right to make that decision for us.

A great deal has changed over the past few years, but

coming out is still one of the most important turning points in the lives of most lesbians and gay men. Although there are exceptions to these generalizations, those born prior to World War II tended to come out to only a few select people and, even then, often only later in life. The baby boomers tended to come out in their late 20s and early 30s. They usually come out to more people, but, often, they still exercise discretion, especially at work and with older relatives. Those born since the 1960s, though, have busted the closet doors down. They often come out as adolescents and sometimes in a way that ensures that the whole world knows. That is much more frequently true in urban areas than in rural ones, but their openness would have been inconceivable just a couple of decades ago.

It should be noted that coming out is frequently a different experience for people of color and for women. Again, generalizations are risky, but it is fair to say that the more socially oppressed and disempowered a person is the greater the risks. That is to say, white men tend to be promoted faster and compensated better than women and people of color. Therefore, white males have some built-in advantages. Some might argue that they have more to risk, but the truth is that their gender and race have not already handicapped them in the race of life.

Regardless of whom we are, when or how we do it, the coming out experience can be painful and traumatic. It is also almost always transformational. Coming out is an act of self-liberation that has few parallels in our lives. It is an act of self integration that seldom happens without long years of therapy.

Coming Out Inside

Before we can integrate anything, though, we have to be fully honest with ourselves. We must come out completely to ourselves first . Most of us cannot remember the initial queer feelings that we had, but we can often remember the first time we got a label to put on those feelings. I remember in junior high school when some boys called one of my best friends a fairy. They meant that he was gay, but the word was so much less harsh than queer or faggot that he embraced it and accepted it as true. It was many years before he fully came out, but, in a real sense, he never fully returned to the closet. Most of us can remember the moment when we admitted in our own heart that we were probably "one of them."

It seems that the earlier in this century we were born, the harder this first stage is to pass through. Then, in order to give sexual expression to our orientation, we must come out to at least one other person. In too many instances we (especially men) did this by getting drunk or participating in anonymous sex. Despite how unhealthy the initial circumstances may have been, once we crack the closet door open, it is nearly impossible to completely close it again.

Coming out to family and friends is almost as difficult as coming out to ourselves. Once we reach a certain level of internal honesty, most of us develop a near obsession for revealing the truth to the people to whom we are close. Our fear often keeps that from happening easily or quickly, but that does not lessen the internal pressure we feel.

In my case, I was in the middle of considering the best strategy to use with my own family when an episode occurred that took matters out of my hands. I had been pastor of the United Methodist church where my parents attended. That reality was going to make this difficult for them on lots of levels. If my sexual orientation became widely known, they would feel embarrassed in their small town, since I had decided to come out of the Methodist church as well as out of the closet. I knew my home church, which had supported my ministry for many years, eventually would have to find out. Perhaps it was a good thing I did not know the half.

In 1981, enough members of the United Methodist Church of which I was the Associate Pastor discovered that I was gay to make my departure imminent. I had never really hidden the fact, and many had known all along. When some very wealthy men in the church discovered it, however, my time with the Methodists was up. I went from being a United Methodist minister to being a pastor in the Metropolitan Community Church. One night, in early 1982, my phone rang about three o'clock in the morning. The Atlanta police were calling to say that the Metropolitan Community Church where I was associate pastor had been broken into and someone needed to come and secure the building.

When I arrived, I discovered that it was much more than just a break-in. The culprits had ransacked my office and spray-painted swastikas and other epithets on the sanctuary walls. There was little I could do about this in the middle of the night, so I boarded up the broken doors as best I could and went home to get some sleep.

About 5:30, the phone rang again. This time, the police were calling to report that the church was on fire. When I arrived, in addition to the police and fire departments, there were also members of the media present. I answered their questions with little thought of the consequences. As a result, I came out on the front page of the Sunday edition of the Atlanta Journal and Constitution. Suddenly, the whole world knew my story.

The consequence was several years of estrangement from my biological family. Almost as painful was the fact that not a single friend from the first 25 years of my life ever contacted me, and very few have had anything to do with me since that day. I would not recommend coming out in the media as a preferred first step.

However you do it, I do recommend coming out. The cost of the closet is almost always greater in the long run than the cost of coming out. Sometimes, we are like the little boy who owned a dog whose tail was supposed to be cut off. The boy was afraid of the puppy being hurt, so he begged his parents to let him be the one to cut the dog's tail. They were doubtful that he could do it, but he was so insistent that they agreed and did not think any more about it until the dog died a few days later.

"What happened?" the boy's mother asked.

"I don't know," said the boy. "I was very careful. I was afraid of hurting him, so I just cut it off a little piece at a time."

Someone who comes out as an openly lesbian or gay person often pays a high price. Even today the person could lose their job. Estrangement from family is a risk. The cost of the closet is more subtle and insidious. Make no mistake; the closet can destroy a life more extensively than losing a job or becoming alienated from loved ones. A closeted individual can never be the happy, healthy or holy person God has called them to be. To grow toward wholeness we must all be honest with ourselves, our God and the significant people in our lives.

Many of us have testimonies not only to the power found in coming out, but also to the need for support when we choose to take that step. You can call the Cathedral of Hope for the location of the church nearest you. There are also several other religious support groups like Dignity for Catholics, Integrity for Episcopalians and Affirmation for United Methodists. An organization called PFLAG (Parents and Friends of Lesbians and Gays) might have a chapter in your city that could provide support for your family and friends.

It is important to remember that the people closest to us are, in a sense, also coming out. They have known us for a while and now have to shift some of the assumptions they have made about us. It is easy to understand that they may feel deceived or, at the very least, a little naive. The consequence may be that the very people on whom you have always relied for love and support might be emotionally unavailable for a time. Hopefully that time will be brief and will pass, but do not be surprised that they too must grapple with this significant fact you have just disclosed to them.

If you do not find support in one of the places listed above, please find support somewhere. You are not alone, though it can feel that way when you are temporarily cut off from your usual support. Allow some of us who had help in coming out to return the favor.

If you have already come out, remember your own struggle and please be willing to be there for someone else who is going through a challenging time. Being honest about one's sexuality is vital for mental and spiritual health. Still, it can be frightening, so do not forget there is one person who has known for years that you are gay: God. Who you are is no surprise to the God who made you and who is proud of the good work.

Support networks, lesbian and gay churches, and other organizations have transformed many lives. They are, even now, transforming how our society deals with lesbian and gay people. As you may know, on June 27, 1969, the New York City police raided the Stonewall Inn, a gay bar in Greenwich Village. There was nothing unusual about the raid. Various law enforcement officials often used similar techniques to harass lesbian and gay people when they gathered. A small group of mostly transvestites and hustlers decided that they had taken enough abuse from the NYPD. We cite the resulting riots as the beginning of the lesbian and gay community's attempt to throw off the blanket of oppression that has long tried to suffocate our lives.

There had been resistance before Stonewall, but this time something was different. This time, the defiance began to spread to other places around the country. The question remains, what made this resistance different? Why did Stonewall spark a revolution? One important factor that enabled this moment of resistance to begin a reform movement was that the lesbian and gay community had begun a grassroots organization that would eventually have chapters in every major city in America.

You see, nine months before Stonewall, on October 6, 1968, the Rev. Troy Perry established the Metropolitan Community Church in Los Angeles. In addition to being a denomination reaching out to lesbian and gay people, it proved to be a catalyst for the founding of hundreds of other diverse lesbian and gay organizations. From the living room of one home, a denomination was born that now has churches in every major city in America and dozens of foreign countries. Many mainline denominations now also have at least one congregation where lesbian and gay people are welcome in every major city. The United Church of Christ and Unitarian Churches both have taken positions that welcome all people, though not every congregation within those denominations is quite as including.

The Christian Church is often cited as a barrier to healthy attitudes toward lesbian and gay people. Much of our internalized homophobia has religious roots. Coming out was complicated for many of us because of our church experiences. I think it is divinely paradoxical that a church has been a major instrument for facilitating the liberation of lesbian and gay people. The mainstream Church has been in the forefront of the oppression of homosexuals, so it is only fitting that God should raise up a unique church to enable our liberation. The justified anger of the lesbian and gay community against religion has often caused people of faith and religious organizations within the lesbian and gay community to be scorned, ridiculed and ignored.

Over the years, we have come to call the celebration of the anniversary of Stonewall's liberating spark our "pride" celebration. Lesbian and gay pride is a recovery of a sense of value rooted in whom we truly are. It is absolutely essential that we recover our sense of being valued, and valuable, as an antidote to the poison of homophobia and shame.

One year, the Atlanta Lesbian and Gay Pride Parade marched to the steps of the State capitol. I had the privilege of being the keynote speaker that year. As a result of that honor, I lost my job as an educational therapist, as well as some friends. One of them said to me, "I just don't understand why we should have lesbian and gay pride." It still astonishes me how deeply lesbian and gay people have internalized homophobia.

A reporter, writing in D magazine, once commented that the "A-gays" do not tend to attend the Cathedral of Hope because it is "too gay." By that, the author meant that our being openly proud to be God's lesbian and gay children kept people with money, power and position from attending. Although it is only partially true, it is completely sad. Like racism, when homophobia is subtly internalized, it is all the more insidious and devastating. Our own internalized shame takes away our power or causes us to use it in ways that are destructive to ourselves and to one another.

God was the first one to look at all creation and to pronounce it good, very good. When you look around at what God has done—how no two flowers or fish or stones are alike—you have just got to believe that God must think the word "queer" is a compliment. Believing this truth with all our hearts can take away the power of those who would ridicule our uniqueness and give us unimaginable inner power. As lesbian and gay Christians, we have the capacity to be proud of who we are or to be ashamed. We can respond from either place in any situation.

If we respond with pride, we respond with power. If we respond with shame, we respond destructively and give away our power. I must admit that this is a lesson I am still learning. Several years ago, I went to the YMCA to play racquetball. I was changing clothes, and the locker room was full of the members of a swim class for older men. Now, these were really older men. When they took their clothes off, it was scary. I had no idea that bones could wrinkle. These guys had wrinkled wrinkles. I could not imagine any of them swimming very far. This one fellow who walked with a cane and was at least 150 pounds overweight told me with pride that he had just finished swimming 750 miles.

I guess he noticed the stunned look on my face, because he said, "I didn't swim it all today. I've been swimming here since I retired 20 years ago." Then he added, "I figured I needed to lose some weight before I get old." He won my complete admiration.

As I was about to leave the locker room, he asked me, in front of everyone, what my t-shirt meant. For a second, I panicked. I thought maybe I was wearing my "Honorary Lesbian" T-shirt, but I wasn't. Then, I realized I was wearing a shirt I'd given my spouse, Bill, that said "2qt2bstr8" (Too Cute To Be Straight).

I tried to brush off his question, but he would not give up. Finally, I stammered something incoherent and made my escape. My racquetball opponent asked, "Why didn't you just tell him what it meant?"

"Well," I said, "I didn't want to give him a heart attack."

The truth is that I responded out of shame rather than out of pride. Why? What did I have to lose? My boss knew I was gay. The whole world knew I was gay. Why should I care if this man knew? Is it possible that if I had responded as a person who was proud of being all that God made me that I might have helped his relationship with his lesbian granddaughter or gay neighbors? Until we stop acting as if we are ashamed, we cannot rationally expect other people to stop treating us shamefully.

Living in every moment and acting at every opportunity without shame takes courage, but it also takes power away from our oppressors. Their words and threats are hollow if there is no shame in us to give them power. The heroes of this life are not people who lived their lives without fear; they are people who counted the cost, felt the fear, and did it anyway. Their pride in who God made them gave their lives power, and they used that power to make the future better for those who were to come after them.

These leaders have paid a price for their actions. I am not such an idealist as to believe that we can live with pride without paying a price. I, too, have lost jobs and friends and even my church. I have had my tires slashed, the paint scratched off my car, my office ransacked, my churches firebombed. Hardly a week goes by without a death threat or hateful letter. But there is one thing I have learned the hard way: the price tag for living with pride as an openly gay or lesbian person isn't nearly as high as the price of living with shame.

In the end, being ashamed of who God made us to be will cost us everything. It will also be very costly for those who will come after us, because they will have to pay the price all over, as if our struggles counted for nothing. It is time to stop the double taxation of the evil of shame. It is time for lesbian and gay Christians to come out with pride.

What follows are some materials that might be helpful if you are coming out to family or friends. Although it is impossible to predict how someone will react to our coming out, it is important that we exercise patience. When people react badly it hurts a great deal, yet remember how long it took you to come to grips with the truth. Our family and friends have been subject to the same homophobic bigotry that we were.

Someone once said, "Everyone is a damned fool for fifteen minutes every day. The secret is not to exceed your limit." It may seem as though our family and friends are exceeding their limits, but if we can be patient and kind they may well discover for themselves just what fools they are being.

That is not to say that you must simply take their abuse or be complicit in their dysfunction. After their initial negative reaction, I didn't see much of my family for several years. That space was painful for all of us but probably necessary for healing to take place. Today we have a healthier relationship than ever. It is the mutual relationship of adults who choose to be together and accept one another's differences as gifts, not as faults. There are lots of resources available to you if you are just coming out or if you are coming out to parents or friends:

- The classic book on the subject is *Coming Out: An Act of Love* by Rob Eichberg. Rob is a clinical psychologist and is involved in National Coming Out Day and The Experience. His book is quite readable, using letters and testimonies to make his points.

- My favorite book title is *There Must Be Fifty Ways to Tell Your Mother* by Lynn Sutcliff. The book consists almost entirely of coming out stories that can be quite inspiring for someone needing reinforcement.

- *Now That You Know* is another book that has been around a while. Written by Betty Fairchild and Nancy Hayward, it was first published in 1979. It has since been updated with some information about AIDS and the family. The subtitle is "What every parent should know about homosexuality." There is one chapter that deals with religion, since that is often the roadblock to many parents' acceptance.

- Another book that might be of help is *A Family and Friend's Guide to Sexual Orientation* by Bob Powers and Alan Ellis. Alan has a PhD in psychology, and Bob was formerly the head of corporate training at AT&T. This combination makes the book interesting in both content and format. I particularly liked the section entitled "101 Steps on the Road to Acceptance."

- Another book, first published in the late 1970s, is *Loving Someone Gay* by Don Clark. Don is a clinical psychologist, and his book has helped hundreds of people with whom I have talked over the years. The revised and updated edition that was published in 1987 is a stronger book.

- *Beyond Acceptance* was written by three parents of lesbian and gay people who are involved in PFLAG (Parents and Friends of Lesbians and Gays). Carolyn Griffin and Marian and Arthur Wirth talk about their own experiences. Many parents have found this helpful.

- If those to whom you are coming out are from strong Christian backgrounds, you might give them a copy of this book or perhaps *Is the Homosexual My Neighbor?* There are several books listed in the back that you might turn to if the Bible is the hang-up. Be careful that you do not disregard their belief system. For example, if they are evangelicals, giving them a book by Bishop John Spong probably would complicate matters. On the other hand, if they are from a Roman Catholic background, you may want to give them a copy of Father John McNeil's book *The Church and the Homosexual*.

- If they are unlikely to read a book, the Cathedral of

Hope has video and audio tapes available. There is also a tape series entitled "Accepting Your Lesbian or Gay Child" produced by PFLAG that contains the stories of parents. That should be a safe bet. If a short brochure that deals with the scriptures would be helpful, one may be obtained from our church.

I have provided some additional material below that also might be of use. Please feel free to reproduce this in any way that is helpful. Sharing the material might help the people to whom you are coming out. Understanding and believing the material will definitely help **you**.

Now You Know

You are probably reading this because someone you care about has come out to you. Perhaps the last thing you feel like doing right now is celebrating. That is understandable and very common, because, on some level, most people grieve when they discover that someone they love is lesbian or gay.

In your more rational moments, you know that the person who has come out to you is still the very same person you have always known and loved. She/he has not changed. All that has changed is what you know about them. The information you have may stir in you many different feelings. Let's talk about some of them.

Grief

Your loved one has not died. Unless they told you about their orientation because they have AIDS, they are not terminally ill. Even if they do have AIDS, the current treatments hold great promise for a long and productive life. So, why are you experiencing this overwhelming feeling of grief?

In a very real sense, there is a part of the person you have always known that has died. Regardless of how you feel about homosexuality, there is still a sense of loss. Like any grief experience, you will go through various stages before you reach acceptance. There will be times when you feel you have made great progress, but then something will happen that will make you feel like screaming.

At times like this, remember that God has given us one another to love, **not** to fix or control. Our role in any relationship is to love unconditionally. If you have just learned that one of your children is lesbian or gay, it is all the more important that you remember that they are still your child. Yes, you have lost something that you **thought** you once had. Eventually you will discover that you have also gained something. Most parents eventually discover that the very traits they treasure about their children are rooted in their sexual orientation.

One young man recalled:

All my life I overheard my parents and grandparents talking about how "special" I was. I think they meant that, as a child, I was gentle, kind, sensitive and tenderhearted. I was also "tough as nails" when I needed to be. All of these traits, I now know, were rooted in my sexual orientation. These were traits of my life long before I entered puberty, so they had nothing to do with sex, only with a natural tendency for which I did not have a word.

Yes, you have lost some hopes and dreams, but, as you move closer to acceptance and unconditional love, you will discover that you have also gained many things in the long run.

Grieve, but remember what the Bible says:

Weeping may endure for the night, but joy comes in the morning.

Psalms 30:5

Guilt

If you are a parent, you probably already have asked yourself, "What did I do wrong?" The answer is simple: **Nothing.** At least you didn't do anything that made your child a homosexual. Sure, you made mistakes. What parent hasn't? But none of those mistakes resulted in your son or daughter being gay. Medical science has accumulated a great deal of evidence that a person's sexual orientation is genetically rooted. You are no more to blame for a child's sexuality than you are "to blame" for their eye color or their handedness. About 10 percent of all people are born left-handed. No one really knows why. At one time, people were forced to use their right hand, and "lefties" were considered inferior because they were different from the vast majority. We now know better, and someday everyone also will know better about sexuality.

Your loved one is different. That is not a sin or a crime. You have nothing about which to feel guilty. You did nothing wrong, and neither did they.

Shame

It feels a lot like guilt, but shame is related to our embarrassment with others who know or might discover our secret. It is true that there is still a great deal of homophobia in our society. It is also true that most of us worry too much about what others think. This may be why it took so long for your loved one to come out to you. They were worried about what you would think.

Much of our shame is based on what society says. Think for a moment about how often society has been wrong in the past. The majority once supported slavery, and the righteous leadership once crucified Jesus. Most of what society has long believed about homosexuality is simply incorrect. Don't let your fear of what others might think cause you to lose someone you love.

Sin

The first reaction of many Christians to learning that a loved one is lesbian or gay is that what they are doing is a sin. Let's talk about that a bit.

First, they did not tell you what they were doing; they told you **who they are**. How can having feelings and attractions you did not choose to have be a sin? If people are, in fact, born lesbian or gay, then what they told you when they came out was the truth about who God made them. How can it be wrong for them to tell you the truth about something they did not choose or decide? With the hatred, oppression and discrimination in our society, no one would simply make the decision to be lesbian or gay. It is simply who they are. How can that be a sin?

Secondly, no, the Bible does **not** call homosexuality a sin. Yes, Leviticus and the Apostle Paul condemn **certain** homosexual acts. But the Bible condemns thousands of heterosexual acts. Does that make heterosexuality a sin? What did Jesus say about homosexuality? Go back and read the Gospels. You will find Jesus warning against judging other people, but **nowhere** will you find him condemning homosexuals.

Yes, homosexuals are sinners in need of redemption, but no more or less than heterosexuals. We **all** must rely on the unconditional grace of God. Do you think homosexuality is stronger than God's grace? No. The Bible says that nothing can separate us from the love of God. That includes our sexuality.

So why do so many preachers say it is such an awful sin? Only they can answer that question, but in the 1960s many of these same preachers were railing against integration and mixing the races. In the '70s and '80s they talked about how the Soviet Union was the "evil empire" about which the Bible warned. Now, it is homosexuals who are the enemy.

Just over a century ago, churches quoted the Old Testament and Paul to justify slavery. Early in the 20th Century, they took scriptures out of their context to oppress women and deny them the right to vote. They were wrong then, and they are wrong now. The Quakers were the first church to condemn slavery, and, more than 100 years ago, they were the first church to say that sexual orientation was no more a sin than being left-handed.

Now you know something that previously you might have only suspected. That is all that has changed. Don't allow that information to rob you of a friend or a member of your family. Those relationships are all too rare and valuable. By coming out to you, they have said how much they value you and trust you. It is obviously important to them that you know who they really are. If you can accept them, you may discover that they will someday have the grace to accept you and love you just as you are. That is something we all need at some point in our lives.

Sample Coming Out Letter

Dear Mom and Dad:

There is something I have wanted to tell you for a long, long time. I know it would be better if we could have this conversation in person. Please forgive me for lacking the courage. I love you and value your love so much that I have been reluctant to risk its loss.

On some level, you may already know this, but I need to be honest enough to say it to you directly. I am lesbian/gay.

I don't know how you are feeling right now, and I wish we didn't live in a world where this information is seen as bad news. The truth is I have struggled for many years to deny, repress and hide this fact. For as long as I can remember I have known that I was different. Long before I even knew what sexual feelings were I sensed that there was something about me that was not like most of the other girls/boys.

It took me a long time to realize that being lesbian/gay isn't about sex. Yes, it is about who I am attracted to, but it is also about a fundamental difference in who I am as a person. I've discovered that much of what people always liked about me is connected to that difference.

You probably have many questions, and I will be glad to answer any of them that I can. You may be very upset right now. Most parents react with grief. It took me a long time to work through my own grief. This isn't something either of us should be ashamed of, but it is obviously something people often feel negatively about. That alone is a source of grief.

Take your time to sort through all of this, and if you need to talk to someone there is _____.
Their phone number is _____. I also have some books, brochures and tapes if that might be helpful.

I want to give you all the time and space you need to begin dealing with this, but, as you might imagine, I'll be on pins and needles until I hear from you. Please know that I understand that this is tough. I will be praying for you.

I hope you know that this has been tough on me, too. This is the hardest letter I have ever written. I did not tell you about this to hurt you. I love you so much that I had to be honest. My only desire is that we have a healthier relationship because you now know the truth. That will probably take some time, but I am willing to work on it.

Love,

I was born in 1939 from Amish ancestry. I knew there was something different about me before I ever started school, but not what. By the time I was out of high school, I knew I had to hide everything about me. I was encouraged to get married. I moved away from home and had my fling. I then moved back close to home. I continued to be pressured to get married. I finally did and lived the straight life. I worked as a coal porter and an evangelist for several churches, but something was missing. After my family grew up, I left. They have nothing to do with me anymore. I met Cece and visited CoH with her. It was totally different there. I felt at home. No more being put down. It was after I started attending CoH that God really came into my life. My life is complete now, even though my children won't have anything to do with me. I really feel the strong presence of God in my life now. I owe it all to God and CoH.

Judy Hedrick
Dallas, TX

Chapter 9
Family Valued

A generation ago no one had ever heard the term "dysfunctional family." Now we either have one or are one. In most cases it is both. We all came from families where we were inadequately and insufficiently loved and valued. For all too many of us the dysfunction was severe, abusive and violent. An alarmingly high percentage of people in my congregation seem to have come from abusive families.

I have read studies suggesting that it was that very abuse that caused these people to be lesbian or gay. While one could draw that conclusion, I think it is incorrect. I know a number of abusive situations that produced heterosexual children. Then there are many persons, like myself, who, though we are homosexual, did not grow up in particularly abusive or dysfunctional families.

Based strictly on my pastoral experience with thousands of gay men and lesbians, I have come to believe that the high rate of abuse often was the **result** of their orientation rather than being the **cause** of their orientation. Parents and siblings sense early on when a child is "different." The abuse often grows out of an attempt to force the child to conform or to punish the child for being different. A great deal of the abuse grows out of parents' shame or guilt. They are determined that they will not have a homosexual child.

Child abuse and neglect is much more complex a subject than I can deal with here, but I want to make two important observations. The first is that it is a complete lie that homosexuals are more likely to abuse children.

Even Tim LaHaye in his homophobic book *The Unhappy Gay* acknowledges that, "The sexual molestation of children is more often perpetrated by heterosexuals than homosexuals." Statistics have proven repeatedly that gay people are responsible for less than 10 percent of child abuse and neglect. As a father of two girls, I am much more comfortable having them cared for by lesbians or gay men than by heterosexual men, who are statistically by far the most dangerous. Why isn't our society afraid of them? They are responsible for most of the child abuse, almost all of the rapes, and an overwhelming percentage of the murders, robberies, war and economic exploitation in the world. Banning homosexuals from being teachers, Scout leaders and other such positions is rank, unsubstantiated bigotry. Homosexuals are not child abusers, at least no more so than the general population. Heterosexual men pose the greater danger.

The other concern that must be stated is that lesbian and gay children are more likely to be abused than heterosexual children. If you are one of us who suffered such abuse, it is vital to understand that you are not alone and that it was not your fault! You were not to blame, regardless of what the abusing adult may have said or done. Do not continue to suffer in silence and shame; find someone you can talk to about the abuse so that you can begin the healing process of recovery.

It is ironic that so much of the popular, "family values" talk originates in very religious, often fundamentalist, families and churches. In my counseling, I have discovered that a disturbingly high percentage of people abused as children grew up in strict religious homes. The ravaging effect of this abuse is no less sinister and despicable than the atrocities the Nazis performed in the name of religion. "Family values" is often just a code phrase for oppressing people who do not fit some contrived pattern. It serves much the same function that "states' rights" served in opposing racial integration in the 1960s. It is simply a concocted moral cover that attempts to justify denial of equal rights to lesbian and gay taxpayers.

Homosexuals come from families, **and** we create our own families. That is something we need to address as lesbian and gay Christians. How do we form families for our unique situation? Do we simply try to replicate heterosexual family patterns that do not appear to be working very well for them? Lesbian and gay folks have a splendid opportunity to reinvent the idea of family in a way that is healthy and liberating. These must be functional families, families of choice and families of faith. Let's look at each of these aspects of our new familial relationships.

Functional Families

The term "dysfunctional family" originated when counselors began dealing with adults who grew up in alcoholic families. There was an awareness that the dynamics in a family where one person was an alcoholic impacted the non-alcoholic members in ways that often hindered their ability to function as happy, healthy human beings. Adult children of alcoholics often shared common struggles and pain. Support groups were formed that followed the Twelve Steps of Alcoholics Anonymous. Al-Anon groups started to support family members of alcoholics. There, they could share their stories and find support.

As different people began talking about their stories, they realized that they had much in common. There were several ways that alcoholism had robbed them of relational skills, though they themselves were not alcoholic. There was an accidental discovery that brought a great deal of light to many people. People who were adult children of alcoholic parents began to talk about what they were discovering about the roots of their dysfunction. As they did, people whose families were not alcoholic discovered that they shared many of the same issues.

A key purpose in this life is to learn how to relate to others. We spend this life learning to talk honestly, feel intimately, and trust confidently. We will spend the next life using those skills in an eternal relationship with God. I am not surprised that God wants us to learn to be authentic before we have to spend an eternity together.

Honesty, intimacy and trust are three crucial and necessary elements of any healthy, long-term, substantial relationship. The family is the place where we are **supposed** to learn the skills required to talk honestly, feel intimately, and trust confidently. Unfortunately, families are often the last place we learn to do those things. While growing up, we too often learned not to talk about things that were important. Every family has its "secret." This is especially true for families where a parent was addicted or compulsive or mentally ill or absent. Rather than talk about the problems of the family, the subject became taboo. Just as most families did not talk about sexual issues, few families discussed their feelings about these kinds of things.

Most of us never learned to talk honestly in our families of origin. Instead, we learned to deny or repress our real feelings. When you said "I hate my brother/sister," a parent usually said, "You don't hate your sister/brother. It's wrong to say that." So it is that you learned to deny and distrust your feelings. You might have heard, "There is nothing to be afraid of. You shouldn't be such a sissy." You didn't stop being afraid; you just stopped acknowledging your fear. "Stop crying; you're acting like a baby. It's time for you to grow up" implied that there was something wrong with feelings of sadness. So it goes.

By distrusting our feelings on other issues, it became

difficult for most of us to recognize, own and trust our feelings about sexual issues. In particular, if we were people who grew up in religious families, we learned, very effectively, to mask, deny, repress and re-label our lesbian or gay feelings. Coming out does not automatically reverse that process. It will still take most of us many years to become healthy enough to acknowledge and deal with intimate feelings.

Trust is the rarest of experiences under the best of circumstances. We are "supposed" to learn to trust in our families. Instead, we heard our parents say one thing and saw them do another. Most damaging, we heard them say that they loved us, but then they would forget their promises, say things that hurt us, or physically inflict pain on us. It became clear, very early, that we could do things that would make them love us less, or at least act like they did. The fear began to grow in our hearts that, if our families knew the truth about us, they would stop loving us altogether. That fear still controls many of us and blocks us from learning to trust.

These three crucial relationship skills go unlearned in the family. As a matter of fact, we usually learned the opposite lessons. Then, as adults, we build all our relationships on the faulty foundation laid by our families of origin. Many of us grew up in families that were very dysfunctional. All of us grew up in families that were flawed and imperfect. Most of us grew up in families that were more unhealthy than we remember.

Now, let me say that the purpose of all of this is not to affix blame; that accomplishes nothing. Although you may have a hard time believing this, I hope you will try: whoever it was that hurt you was doing the best they could with the health and skill they had at that time. That does not mean they were right or that what they did was good. It simply means that they, too, were acting out of their own pain, brokenness and dysfunction.

They were damaged, and they damaged us. But we accomplish little by blaming them for our current problems. It is important to get to the roots, but, beyond that, we must take responsibility and make the necessary changes to get well. If all we do is find out the source of our dysfunction, we may be worse off rather than better.

Recovery from family-rooted dysfunctions is laborious. It requires transformation at the deepest level. Recovery is a process, and time is a crucial element in that process. We learned dysfunctional patterns of relating early in our lives, and we have been repeating them over and over and over. Breaking that pattern and establishing new ones can happen. It will not be easy, and it will not happen instantly. Recovery is not magic. It takes time, and it is painfully hard work. As John Fortunato, author of *Embracing the Exile: Healing Journeys of Gay Christians*, says about therapy, "The bad news is that you don't die." The good news is that you can recover. In Ezekiel 36:26, God says:

> *I will give you a new heart and put a new spirit in you; I will remove from you your heart of stone and give you a heart of flesh.*

God is both a loving Father and a nurturing Mother who can heal us of wounds inflicted by our earthly family. Only when we recover from our dysfunctional families can we create new functional ones.

Families of Choice

Many of us do not have the luxury of family members who care enough about us to encourage us to share who we really are. Our biological families have abandoned or abused many of us. Probably most of us have dishonest, distant or unhealthy relationships with our families because we are lesbian or gay. Although our sexual orientation is not something we chose, it still seems our families are punishing us for it. The loss of family is painful. To be abused or abandoned by the very people we expected would love and support us is a source of real loneliness for many of us. To have to live a lie or distance ourselves from the people who should know us best can wound our self-esteem. Having that kind of dysfunctional family experience can lead to addictions or impair all our other relationships.

Lesbian and gay people face the daunting challenge of redefining the concept of family. This is also an incredible opportunity. We can create families free from the arbitrary rules and limitations of the nuclear family that seem to be the litmus test of orthodoxy for the Religious Right. We can include in our new families people who enrich our lives rather than just those with whom we share some common genetic material.

At one time, church growth experts said that pastors should not use the term "family" when talking about the church. The problem, they maintained, was that when we called our congregations families, it gave everyone the message that they were supposed to act out the dysfunctions of the families in which they were raised.

All over this country, we see most denominations fighting like children over who gets the bigger piece of pie. This kind of dysfunction is not limited to the Church. If you are involved in other groups in the lesbian and gay community, you have seen what happens when two or more gather together. Even in the workplace, dynamics soon develop that cause us to resemble a dysfunctional family. The temptation is to give up on the idea of family completely. Yet we have seen what has happened in the inner cities of this nation when community and family connections were abandoned. And most of us have already discovered that no matter how anxious we are to let go of our family ties, it seems that they will not let go of us.

We all need to be a part of a family, but it must be a functional family. The lesbian and gay community, and our society at large, needs to create new, healthy, supportive and life-giving families. Those new families may include our biological family members if they wish it and if they can be supportive and life-giving. If not, then we must release them to live their lives while we move forward to live ours. In South Georgia we used to say, "You can't teach a pig to sing. It wastes your time, and it irritates the pig." Sometimes that is how it is with biological family members. They do not have the capacity or the inclination to change their faith systems, so we need to stop wasting our time and irritating them. We need to get on with the job of forming our own functional families of choice.

Love must be unconditional, and our biological families may not have the capability to give us that kind of love. Instead of allowing that inability to paralyze us, we need to deliberately begin to create new families for ourselves, and we need to become families for one another.

Children cannot select their families, but healthy adults can take responsibility for their own lives. As adults we can choose our own family. It is wonderful when we can include our biological families as a part of our chosen families as well. Creating healthy new families sounds like a good idea, but how do we do it?

First, I must stress that it will not happen by accident. It must be something we consciously and deliberately choose to create. It requires a great investment of time. In our generation, time is the currency of real value. If we are going to create valuable relationships, we must invest our time with the people we wish to have as our family. That does not mean we have to spend all of our free time together, but it does mean that our lives must become intertwined sufficiently so that a bond forms that is strong and dependable. It means doing things together that are fun, and it means sharing serious and painful times as well. It must become a priority for us. We are all busy people, but nothing we do is more important than spending time with our families.

The second thing I invite you to notice about our new families is that they value diversity. Although it is important that we share common core values, what makes these new families such a source of joy is that each person brings a different color to the family portrait we are painting. In a dysfunctional family, everyone must conform, think alike, act alike, share the same values. Communities that value this kind of uniformity usually end up like fundamentalist churches or organizations such as the Ku Klux Klan. Differences threaten a dysfunctional family, but a healthy family treasures diversity. We celebrate what we have in common, but we do not try to force conformity.

Families of Faith

One other factor in creating healthy families is that we share a common faith. Now, that does not mean that we all believe exactly the same things. The new lesbian and gay families I have witnessed that are functional and life-giving contain members of very serious faith, though they may never attend church. They are people who share a common value system in which "self" and "self-gratification" are not the supreme values. Lesbian and gay people seldom rear children and are often excluded from, or uncomfortable with, biological families. As a result, the contemporary religion of "self-ism" can easily ensnare them. Still, I have witnessed extraordinary acts of self-giving love by lesbian and gay people. The AIDS crisis has produced an army of heroes.

In Matthew 12:46-50, there is an interesting story in which Jesus' mother and brothers had come to get him and take him home. They thought he had gone off the deep end and was making a fool of himself. Jesus points around the room and says:

> *"Who is my mother, and who are my brothers?"*
> *And pointing to his disciples, he said, "Here are*
> *my mother and my brothers! For whoever does the*
> *will of God in heaven is my brother and sister and*
> *mother."*

Jesus was saying that the people who were his family were related to him by faith. These were people Jesus chose to be his family. These were people who shared his values and with whom he chose to share his life.

Many attempts by lesbian and gay people to form new families fail at this point. We often create relationships based on common history or jobs or experiences. If, however, we do not have common values, these new families will be as dysfunctional as our families of origin.

I have a group of friends who had created a strong bond. They played cards together and spent almost every holiday with one another. One person could start a story and another member of the group could finish it. They had so many inside jokes and codes that sometimes outsiders were uncomfortable around them. In the group were two couples and two single guys. Then one of the single guys fell in love.

The group worked very hard to include the new friend in the group, but it soon became clear that it was not working. He, too, sensed it and became increasingly critical of the group. The tension became so great that the group began to do things together without including the new couple. As they discussed the situation among themselves, they tried to honestly identify what had happened. The new person was witty, attractive, well-educated and personable. What they finally realized was that he was also very selfish. His principle concern in every situation was how it impacted him. Although the group had not done so deliberately, what had evolved was a family in which each member was more concerned with the others in the group. The new guy simply did not share their core values. The relationship failed, and their friend returned to the family. Eventually the group did add new members, but they were people who shared enough of their values to make them compatible.

I remember one night, shortly after I came to Dallas, I was sound asleep when the phone rang. It was one of the volunteers staffing our crisis line. Although very apologetic about waking me at three o'clock in the morning, he explained that he had received a call that a guy named Jim was dying at Parkland Memorial Hospital. The family had called and asked if I would come to the hospital. The name did not ring a bell for me, but I was still new to the area. When I got to the room, I did not recognize the man who was dying, but I did recognize the family. They were all members of my church.

They were not physically related to the man at all, but here were five or six women and men who shared the same spirit. They were family in the best sense of that word. You see, a family sticks together when things get tough. Family members love each other in spite of mistakes. Members of a true family may have disagreements, but they share the same spirit.

The lesbian and gay community has a wonderful opportunity to break new ground in redefining the concept of family. Only recently has the word come to mean a husband and wife and 2.4 children. For most of the history of the human race, we have lived together in extended families that were not limited to immediate blood relatives.

In the Gospel of Luke, Jesus was left behind in the temple at the age of 12. Interestingly, Mary and Joseph just assumed that he was with the extended family and did not miss him at first. The healthiest human who ever lived grew up in a family that would not be "traditional" by today's standards. Further, when he was an adult, Jesus created his own family. Jesus' family of choice would assuredly get some strange looks in the suburbs of modern America.

We must choose for our family people who are healthy (or are at least trying to get healthy), people who are authentic, and people with whom we share a common faith and value system. I believe it is a mistake for gay and lesbian people to try to emulate the modern American model of family. Two people do not form a family; they form a couple. There is nothing wrong with that, but everyone needs a family. Many relationships, gay and straight, fail because two people bring too many expectations into the relationship. Our needs are too great for any one person to meet them all. It is unreasonable to expect that one person can fulfill all our emotional, mental, physical, sexual, intellectual, affectional, relational and spiritual needs. That is a perception designed for frustration and failure.

Lesbian and gay people will form couple relationships, but it is important that the couple bring into its circle other people who are capable of mutual caring. Our spouses may meet our primary needs, including our sexual needs, but it is unhealthy for that relationship to become so ingrown that it excludes friends and loved ones with whom we form bonds. Deliberately and consciously creating extended families is essential if lesbian and gay people are going to resist replication of the relational problems seen in the rest of society.

I have tried to talk about how we as lesbian and gay people can be the sons and daughters of God, that is, how we can be holy. We have looked at some issues that can help us be more functional, that is, healthy. In the next two chapters, I want to examine lesbian and gay relationships, hoping that we will also discover how we can be happier.

Many good books are available on lesbian and gay relationships. You will find a list of them in the back of this book. If you cannot find them in your area, you can order them through Sources of Hope Bookstore by calling, toll-free, (800) 501-HOPE (4673).

My intention is not to provide comprehensive guidance for lesbian and gay relationships. I am only offering some insights about how our faith as Christians can affect our relationships. I have deliberately chosen to include illustrations from my own relationship, hoping that they might make some of the material more accessible. In addition, heterosexual couples are so visible that those of us in same-gender relationships who can afford to be open and visible have an obligation to be just that.

I was raised in a very conservative Church of Christ environment. That really says it all. No instrumental music, no movies, no dancing, etc. Basically, no enjoyment of life, yet I knew that Jesus said that I came that you might have life and have it more abundantly.

I first attended Cathedral of Hope in January 1997. I had to use the tissue in the racks on the backs of the pews that very first visit. I've used the tissues many times since, because, with my very first visit, I knew that I was home. The inclusive language and loving environment warmed my soul. I've never regretted coming to CoH, as I felt from day one and still do, that THIS IS WHAT religion and Christianity should be about. I found the love of God here at a predominately gay church here in the buckle of the Bible belt. Yes, right here in Dallas, Texas, I found the inclusive love and acceptance of God.

Jon Harris
Dallas, TX

Chapter 10

A Happy, Healthy, Holy Couple

Like almost every other person—man or woman, straight or gay—I grew up hoping someday to meet someone, fall in love, and live happily ever after. For the first 20 years of my life, I assumed that person would be a woman. When I was only 19, because of a severe shortage of Methodist preachers in South Georgia, I was assigned to pastor a circuit of three small rural churches. It was my first time away from home. The members of my church were all old enough to be my grandparents, and I went through a time of excruciating loneliness. The fact that I was doing a job for which I was in no way prepared only exacerbated my feelings of isolation. I remember spending many nights crying out to God in my loneliness for someone to love who would help make my life complete. Over the years, I dated lots of girls, and later women, but something about those relationships just did not work for me. Eventually, I discovered exactly what was wrong by taking the chance of being honest with myself.

In 1980, after serving as a United Methodist minister for seven years, I decided that I could no longer continue to preach the truth of God and live a lie. Moving to Atlanta, I joined the staff of an inner-city Methodist church, knowing my life was about to make a major change. In Atlanta, I met Jimmy Brock, a pastor who, after 25 years of marriage and a successful career as a Baptist pastor, had just come out of the closet. He and I decided that we should create a support network for ourselves, so we volunteered as counselors for the Atlanta Gay Center Crisis Line.

On Saturday, October 18, 1980, we joined about 15 other men and women at the center to begin six weeks of training. One of the two people leading the training was a man I had never met named Bill Eure. I did not realize it at the time, but God was about to answer my prayers from seven years before.

As the weekly training sessions went along, I realized that, although I was not really learning anything new, I looked forward to each week's session. Both Jimmy and I made several friends in that class, so it was serving our purpose. It also connected us with the lesbian and gay community in Atlanta. One night after class, while everyone was standing around chatting, Bill came over and, out of the blue, asked me if I would like to go to the ballet with him that Friday night. I had never been to the ballet, and since that was something gay men are "supposed" to enjoy, it sounded like fun. It wasn't until the next day that I realized he had asked me for a date. Well, it is fair to say that my life has never been the same. Bill and I became friends, lovers, business partners, companions and spouses. Beyond my relationship with God, Bill has been the best gift I ever received. All these years later, I never fall asleep at night without giving thanks for him and the life we have built together.

I will never forget how nervous I was the first Sunday he attended the Methodist church where I was associate pastor. For the first time, two segments of my life came together in a way they never had before. I think that was true for him as well. When he was young, Bill also felt called to serve God, but he was aware of his sexual orientation much earlier than I was. He knew that ministry was not very likely for a Baptist boy from North Carolina who just happened to be gay. I'm not sure being a pastor's spouse was what he had in mind, but over the years that we have been together, he truly has had quite a ministry.

The journey on which God has led us since that first

date has been a very interesting one. Although it has not always been easy, I can honestly say we have never had a fight or even a serious disagreement. I do not think either of us can imagine our life without the other. When different churches have called me to be their pastor, we have made the decision together. We went as partners and had to be certain that God was calling us both. Although Bill has spent much of his adulthood earning his living as a systems analyst, his life, as much as mine, has been about serving God. I have a degree in psychology and have counseled hundreds of couples over the years, but most of what I believe about relationships grows out of the joy I have found in ours.

My premise that lesbian and gay relationships can be happy, healthy and holy is rooted not in theory, but in my own experience. When a relationship is good, it is a wonderful experience, but it is **not** true that a bad relationship is better than no relationship at all. Clearly, we have several strikes against us, but I think lesbian and gay couples have some advantages as well. Let's look at some liabilities first, then at some assets, and then at some realities of making a relationship work.

Enemies of Lesbian and Gay Relationships

No Role Models

When I met them, Eileen and Sarah had been together more than fifty years. They met in the military during World War II, and, except for a couple of hospital stays, they had never spent a night apart. The first few years they lived together, they did not know that there were any other people in the world like them. Eventually, they connected with a few other couples, but, mostly, they lived quietly in a small town in the mountains of North Georgia. The people at the First Baptist Church there never suspected they had two real live lesbians in their midst. It irritated Sarah a bit that the congregation referred to them as "old maid school teachers."

When they finally came to our church for the first time, they were astonished that there were really other lesbian and gay people who were serious about their faith. They visited us a few times, but then I did not see them again for several months. One day I ran into Sarah at a mall, and she explained that, although they liked it very much, our church just was not home. They had been hidden so deeply in the closet for so long that they had gotten comfortable there. They thought they would just stick with First Baptist.

I understood their decision, but I was also very sorry. My regret was not for Sarah and Eileen, but for us. Our community desperately needs visible role models of relationships that are healthy and durable. These two women were that. Unfortunately, many long-term lesbian or gay couples, like Eileen and Sarah, are virtually invisible. They got together in an era when they believed they had no other option but to hide who they are. They learned to blend in and became comfortable with the life they made.

There are hundreds of couples at the Cathedral of Hope who are in long-term relationships, but I never saw any of them when I was growing up. There were no books or television programs that gave me any hope that two men or two women could live together happily ever after. By and large, I have felt that Bill and I have been making this up as we go along. Frankly, it has been a bit scary to realize that people often look to us as role models. We all need to see, with our own eyes, that our belief that lesbian and gay relationships can work is more than just a dream.

After decades of ministry, in both predominantly heterosexual and predominantly homosexual churches, I have discovered that everyone faces struggles that are remarkably similar. The lack of role models is one of the liabilities that lesbian and gay couples have had to accept. Although that has changed a great deal in my lifetime, I suspect we are still a long way from a successful network series depicting the daily struggles of the modern gay family. Without visible role models, there is a part of our hearts that still believes our relationships are "queer."

The Dating Game

One Sunday morning when I was a senior in high school, I went bopping into my Sunday School class and made a frightening discovery. There, huddled together on the far side of the room, were the six or seven girls who attended that class. They were talking quietly, but a couple of them kept glancing over at me. Suddenly, I had the terrifying realization that I had dated every one of those girls. It was that day I volunteered to teach the third-graders.

I did date a lot in high school, but I do not think anyone ever labeled me promiscuous. We expect teenagers to have a date almost every weekend and think nothing about it if each date is with a different person. Dating is simply a healthy way to practice the relationships we will seek to establish later in life. Perhaps like you, I had a great deal of experience practicing heterosexual relationships, but in the little town in South Georgia where I grew up, opportunities for gay dates were rare.

Most lesbians and gay men never have a chance to "date" until they are adults. Thankfully, that is changing somewhat today, but the reality is that, even in the cases where someone comes out as a teenager, the opportunities for practice are limited. As a result, lesbian and gay people date as adults. Often—perhaps too often—adult dating includes sex. Hence, society has labeled us promiscuous for doing what it deprived us of the opportunity to do when we were teenagers.

In addition, there is little awareness in our own community that we need that practice time. Since we are adults with heterosexuals as our only role models, we sense enormous pressure to find a spouse, settle down and get on with living happily ever after. What results is often a series of short-term relationships, generally lasting two-to-four years.

That produces two negative results. We internalize the end of the relationship as a failure because it did not endure, and we grow cynical about our ability to sustain healthy relationships. We would think teenagers who broke up with their girlfriends or boyfriends were silly if they took that to mean they were losers at love. The other equally unfortunate result is that we establish a pattern of serial monogamy. Heterosexuals are prone to this as well, but since we date almost exclusively as adults, it is of even more concern for us. We tend to go from one relationship to another.

Lesbian and gay people need to learn to date without hearing wedding bells after a few hot flashes. In this case, too, we are like dating teenagers. That is to say, I am probably wasting my breath. You will nod your head, and this newly gained wisdom will last until the next batch of hormones kicks in. Don't say you weren't warned, and don't beat yourself up for what is a natural and normal pattern. Redwood trees live for hundreds of years; lilies bloom for only a day. That does not make redwoods morally superior to lilies. Do not spoil the beauty of a relationship by expecting something from it that was not its nature or by labeling it a failure because it was a flower and not a tree. Take the gifts that each relationship brings and go into the next one as a brighter man or a healthier woman.

Lack of Societal Support

The most obvious liability for lesbian and gay relationships is the fact that we still lack the support and structure our society offers heterosexuals. With a name like Piazza, you might have guessed that my family is Italian and therefore Roman Catholic. My grandparents are immigrants. Divorce was not legal in Italy until the 1960s. As a result, there has never been a divorce in my family. That does not mean there has not been the need for one, but, when a couple begins to have trouble, there is enormous pressure to work it out and stay together.

My grandparents loved me very much, and they adopted Bill into the family. If Bill and I were to have experienced trouble, I could not really have talked to them about it. They would have been as supportive as 90-year-old Italian immigrants could be, and they would have been sad if Bill and I had gone our separate ways after all these years. But they would not have thought it was a sin or a violation of a sacred covenant. After all, we are not legally married.

With one out of every two heterosexual marriages ending in divorce, imagine for a moment what those statistics could be. What would happen if all it took to get a divorce was to call a moving van? Or what if children were not involved? Or what if the heterosexual's family would be relieved if the relationship ended? Considering all of those factors, it is a wonder that any lesbian and gay relationships endure and are healthy.

Moreover, there are the pressures of homophobia, living in the closet, dysfunctional families, AIDS and living in a secular culture, as well as other liabilities that we must face. It is fortunate that there are also some assets that our relationships have, or none of them would endure.

Allies of Lesbian and Gay Relationships

Deeper Intimacy

Finding enemies is always easier than making friends. In the art of relationship building, it is easier to identify all of the things that conspire against us than to discover the advantages we have. The most obvious thing I discovered when I began having relationships with men was that it was easier for me to develop greater intimacy more quickly. The reasons for this are obvious. We were both men, so we shared a great deal more in common. Our relationship, therefore, could get off to a faster start. We communicated more effectively, because we were socialized to speak the same language. More accurately, perhaps, we knew more clearly the meaning behind what we said or did.

Now, I should note that this also can be a liability, since so many relationships never move beyond that initial level of intimacy. I have two friends that spent the first few weeks of their relationship talking long into the night, every night. It was obnoxious to be around them. Soon they moved in together and discovered they had nothing to say to one another. We must be aware of that trap.

If, on the other hand, we do not assume that initial intimacy is sufficient, then lesbian and gay people may have a head start on creating more genuine relationships. This makes sense when you consider that the person you are with already knows the biggest secret of your life. That is a good opportunity to create an honest, open channel of communication for sharing deeper, and, perhaps, more painful secrets. The vulnerability required to be open about one's sexuality, even with just one other person, can be a foundation upon which to build. Although you may have experienced pain in the past when you let your guard down, now you are with someone who has taken that journey as well. Perhaps it is time to take the risk of being more self-disclosing. This kind of honesty can renew even long-term relationships.

Sex

A second advantage lesbian and gay couples have is the opportunity to celebrate our sexuality more fully. All couples, gay or straight, bring a number of sexual issues to bed with them. The advantage that some lesbian and gay couples have is that, by virtue of being a sexual minority and because we have had to, we are more likely to be able to talk about these issues. Communication will not cure them all, but I am comforted by how healing it is for people to be able to talk about sex honestly with someone else. In a day when people are always talking about sex, there is very little genuine communication going on about authentic and important issues regarding it.

Lesbian and gay couples are less likely to be rigid in our sexual expressions with our partners. We do not have a lot of stereotypes about how gay sex works or how it is to be done. No nun ever taught us the right or wrong way for two people of the same gender to have sex. Few of our parents instilled their prejudices or presumptions about lesbian and gay sexual techniques.

We are free to enjoy whatever feels good for us and our partner. Since we share our partner's gender, we have some good clues about what feels good. Like our food and clothing preferences, each person's sexual taste is different, but, at least, we have a common point of reference. In doing premarital counseling for heterosexuals, it was appalling how little men and women knew about their partner's sexual needs. They also had a much tougher time talking about these problems, and solving them was not as likely to occur. It still saddens me that some of my heterosexual friends cannot bring themselves to tell their husbands or wives what they would like to do in bed.

Lesbian and gay couples seem to enjoy sex more often and longer into their relationships. That is a gift that strengthens our relationships and pleases God. We were created by God in such a way that sexual expression feels good and meets a wide range of needs. We may conclude that sexuality is a gift of God intended for our pleasure. Christians should enjoy sex more than atheists because it should be an act of our souls as well as our bodies.

We have the advantage of being free from limits that might make us think that sex is only to be done in the missionary position on Saturday from 10:30 to 10:45 p.m. I hope that you have not allowed the repression of the heterosexual Church to limit your enthusiasm, imagination and creativity. If it is fun, mutual, healthy and responsible, then it is all right with God. The only bad sex is sex that is not fun for both parties or that damages a person physically or emotionally.

Arbitrary values about sex arise more often from unhealthy societal values than from the God of creation. The Bible is not sex-negative, and most of our Victorian ideas about sex do not come from the Bible, but from sexually repressed and repressive people. Most of us grew up in churches that were anti-sexual. That reality still exists in churches today. The result is a truly weird world where the Family Channel (once owned by Pat Robertson and company) would never show two people making love but regularly broadcast genocidal westerns, murder mysteries and war stories. Killing our neighbor is more morally acceptable than loving them. One wonders what the founders of the Family Channel are so afraid of when violence is safer for their souls than sex. Perhaps lesbian and gay Christians can give some leadership in reclaiming sexuality as a gift from God.

Freedom from Role Expectations

Although there are other advantages that lesbian and gay relationships have, there is only one more I will mention here: our freedom from the expectations that are typically placed upon heterosexuals to fulfill particular roles. Despite all of the shows hosted by Oprah and Dr. Phil, most heterosexual men and women still lock themselves into traditional roles. She washes the clothes; he fixes the dryer when it breaks.

When I speak to predominantly heterosexual organizations or classes, I often still have someone ask Bill and me which one of us is the "woman." I always want to challenge them for their narrow-minded assumptions that lesbian and gay relationships are as trapped by limitations as their relationships. While it is true that some gay men are more masculine than others and some lesbians are more feminine, making assumptions about roles on that basis can lead to completely erroneous conclusions.

Bill and I both enjoy cooking, and we both hate washing the dishes. Both of us are competent at household chores, and both of us are rather incompetent when it comes to mechanical repairs. The division of labor for us is based on time, interest and ability, not on which of us is the "man" and which one is the "woman." Because we are freer of those stifling roles, we are forced to negotiate common needs, and the result is much better for the relationship than stereotypical assumptions.

Now, I should probably acknowledge that there are still lesbian and gay relationships that conform to heterosexual roles. This seems particularly true of older couples and of some cultures. Although this type of relationship is not my choice, if it works for them, then that is good. The point is that we are free to choose what kinds of roles work for us and to change those roles as we choose.

Greater intimacy, sexual celebration and being free from the limits of roles provide some advantages that can offset the obstacles to healthy relationships for lesbian and gay people. Still, making any relationship work is a challenge. The only advice I can offer comes from what has worked in our relationship and what I have seen in the healthy relationships within my church. I have made a brief list of the five pieces of advice I offer every new couple I counsel.

- **Pray.** We need all of the help we can get, and relationships are much more likely to succeed if God is a part of them. Beyond the obvious benefit of seeking God's favor, I think praying for your partner and your relationship does something else. Often praying together is tougher and requires more genuine intimacy than making love. When you pray for your relationship, you are framing it in a context of something that has eternal value and something that God values. That shift alone can make all the difference in the world.

  Bill was an answer to my prayers. As Ruth Graham (Billy Graham's wife) said, "Thank God not every prayer is answered, or I would have married the wrong man several times." It is not just beginning prayer; it is sustaining prayer. Many relationships get off to a great start, but few have enduring quality. Because of his work and his nature, Bill gets up much earlier than I do. Conversely, I stay up reading long after he is sound asleep. That has been the pattern for almost every night of our life together. For the past several thousand nights, I have turned off the light, rolled over close and prayed for Bill and for our relationship. He gets up early and does his devotions in the morning, so our relationship gets prayed for at the beginning and end of every day. I do not know if that is what has made it work, but I know it has made us handle it with more care, because we have invited God to be a part of it.

- **Make sacred covenants.** The second piece of advice I would offer is that you make promises that you can keep, and that you keep the promises you make. The one thing David and Jonathan, and Ruth and Naomi had in common was that they made sacred covenants. They were sacred because they involved God and because they were honored.

    People often make promises before they are ready, and in the heat of passion in a new relationship, people make promises they cannot keep. That can be fatal to a relationship and to a person's self-esteem. The Cathedral of Hope does not perform services of Holy Union until a couple has been dating exclusively for at least a year. Although that is an arbitrary time, we recognize the damage done by asking couples to make promises prematurely.

    Make promises you can keep, keep the promises that you make, and some day those promises will keep you. Over the years we have been together, Bill and I have known great stress from outside our relationship. It is tough being so publicly out in the South. Add to the pressure that comes with regular hate-mail and death threats the strain that comes to any family living in a church parsonage. Bill has had to give up jobs, homes, friends and businesses to move with me to new churches. We have twice taken major cuts in income by moving to answer a call. Still, our relationship thrives and is a source of strength and joy for both of us. We have kept our promises to each other, and, in the tough times, our promises have kept us.

- **Communicate.** This is always much tougher than it sounds. After working at church all day, sometimes the last thing I want to do when I get home is concentrate on listening and communicating. Communication, however, does not happen casually or accidentally. When I first came to Dallas, Bill stayed behind to sell our business and our home. We thought it would only take a few weeks, but it took almost a year. During that time, we wrote and talked on the phone every day. As hard as it was to be apart, it was one of the best times of growth for our relationship because we did not leave communication to chance.

- **Laugh and Play.** Don't take it all so seriously. We have friends who are always working on their relationship. It makes me tired just to be around them. Those kinds of relationships almost never last. No one has that kind of energy. Home should be a place that you go to relax and have fun. Although you may not have sex every day or even every week, your relationship will not last long unless you can laugh together on a daily basis. Every week you should do something that is fun. Enjoy each other's company. If you cannot do that start sorting out the underwear; one of you will be moving soon.

- **Hang on.** When people ask how Bill and I have stayed together for more than two-and-a-half decades I often answer, only half jokingly, "Well, we never broke up." All relationships go through tough times. It may be that yours is not fun right now, and maybe you should see a counselor or pastor. There are times when you may need to work on some issues together. There are times when one or the other of you may need to work some issues out alone. That does not mean the relationship is ready to be discarded.

At some point, a relationship hits a wall. For heterosexual couples it usually occurs at seven years, and for gay couples three to five. You should expect that and handle it. You can deal with it in this relationship or the next, or the one after that, but you cannot avoid it. Inevitably you are going to wonder if it is worth it. What you ought to be asking is if it is worth starting over with someone new and still ending up at this exact spot.

Some couples simply hang on and endure this period, and, eventually, it passes. Others choose to work through it, and it passes more quickly and, probably, more constructively. Still others have run from these issues all of their lives, and that is how they will handle them now. I hope that you will not give up, give in or give out too soon. Lesbian and gay people can have happy, healthy and holy relationships.

I once saw an elderly couple going into a store together. Both shuffled slowly, and, for the life of me, I could not figure out if he was leaning on her or she was leaning on him. For a moment, I smiled, thinking that someday Bill and I will be like that. Two little old men shuffling along, arm in arm, leaning on each other. I promise you this: if anyone has anything homophobic to say to us then, I'll just hit them with my cane.

The Cathedral has always been a very powerful place for many people that I know. Great things came from the cathedral, whether they were from sermons, volunteer work, people associated with a group. The Cathedral always felt comfortable. Sunday mornings were a ritual, and they felt a sense of belonging. You know, Psychology 101. Maslow's hierarchy of needs, right? One of those needs was to feel part of a group. What better place, being gay, could you feel part of a group?

With my Catholic background, anytime I was away from the Cathedral I felt an enormous amount of guilt. Maybe I was cheating my soul, not quite sure. Whatever the reason, we, the Christian gay community, had a place to go, for our soul, for our sense of "being" for our passion for Christ.

Kelli Trudel
Colleyville, TX

Chapter 11
AIDS:
Blessings from a Curse

No book of this nature would be complete without talking briefly about Acquired Immune Deficiency Syndrome or AIDS. The Cathedral of Hope has more than 800 people that it is trying to serve who are living with AIDS. Each day that list grows. In 1995, a member of our staff died of AIDS. In the first 10 years of the epidemic, we performed nearly 1,000 funerals.

It seems like just yesterday that I was the assistant pastor of the Atlanta Metropolitan Community Church when the Centers for Disease Control called to ask me some questions about my congregation. I was incredulous when they told me that there was a cancer that seemed to be striking only gay men. I must admit that, although I answered his questions, I thought they were simply mistaken. In 1981, I could not imagine a cancer that would strike only gay men. When they called back some time later to talk to me about something called GRID (Gay Related Immune Disorder), I began to get scared. In my worst nightmare, I could not have conceived such an awful curse descending upon our community.

I have buried hundreds of young men in the prime of their lives, many of whom were my friends, all of whom were my brothers. I have wept and cursed and laughed with them. I have walked out of hospital rooms and slammed my fist against elevator walls in almost every hospital in Atlanta, Jacksonville and Dallas. There have been hundreds of times when I have said "I can't take this any more." The

Rev. Troy Perry, founder of the Metropolitan Community Church, described our church when he said, "We all have AIDS. We have it in our body or in our hearts."

In the early days of this epidemic, the suffering of persons infected with HIV worsened due to callous treatment by the medical community. One of the first members of my church to get sick was a beautiful young man named Jeff. The first time he was in the hospital, I had to go by and see him every day at lunch because the nurse's aides who delivered the meals refused to enter his room. They would lay his lunch on the floor in the hall, though he was too weak to get out of bed and get it himself. I went by every day to make sure he was at least able to eat. Today, things have changed, but in some places treatment is still shoddy.

Although there is still no cure for or a vaccine against AIDS, there have been advances in care and treatment. The development of protease inhibitors in 1995/96 contributed to the recovery of many people. Folks who had gone on disability have returned to work. Many who were living for the moment are now making plans for the future.

The response in our community has been interesting. While one would not expect the unbridled celebration a cure would bring, it is surprising how so much progress has brought so little joy. Like everyone, I grieve for all those friends and loved ones who contracted AIDS too early to be helped. I know there are still many unanswered questions, but the news is good and hopeful.

One of the realities of the good news is that many people who had prepared for death have no skills to now prepare for life. Dreams, goals and plans were shelved or scrapped. What do they do now? One friend had a great job with a promising future. When his T-cells dropped below 200, he "celebrated" by telling his boss off and quitting. Then, five years later, his T-cells had tripled, his viral load was negligible, and his overall health was excellent. He had exhausted his savings and no longer qualified for disability. He suffered from major depression because, as he says, "Death was one promise I assumed life would keep." He was not cured, but neither was he really sick. Given an opportunity to begin again, he didn't know what to do with his life.

As of this writing, it is still too early to report the outcome of his story, but, fortunately, I think he will be all right. He has decided that, while the goal of his first career was to make money, in his new career he hopes to make a difference. AIDS has helped him to change his life's orientation from success to significance. Finding his purpose and mission has been vital to curing his depression and giving quality to his future.

At the Cathedral of Hope, we have had several members who continued to live with HIV long after medical authorities said they should have died. Daryl Smith, who is one of my oldest and dearest friends, was the first person to "come out" to me as HIV-positive after I moved to Dallas in 1987. Daryl has been HIV-positive since 1983. His health is very good, though his T-cell count has been low for years. I credit his long-term survival and good health, in large part, to his faith, his service to others, and the fact that he is so stubborn.

I do not know how medically accurate that assessment is, though I can attest to his stubbornness. I also know that his HIV status has ironically resulted in a higher quality of life for himself and many others. Daryl has allowed his diagnosis to be a source of inspiration to many members of our congregation. For many years, through the worst of the epidemic, he led Ten-Step HELP (Healing Experiences for Living Positively) groups that taught people to live healthily from the inside out with hope. Daryl's story is a powerful testimony, with lessons for people living with AIDS, cancer and other life-threatening illnesses. He writes:

Growing up in a small Texas town, there was not much support for being different. Between my devoutly Baptist mother, who taught me a certain kind of pride that excluded everyone but people just like me, and my redneck father, who bounced between the Baptists and the bottle, I did not have exceptional role models for healthy living.

I always knew I was somehow different from the family raising me. For one thing, I loved old movies and the fantasies they offered. They were an escape, and those old black-and-white films increased my vocabulary and spared me from a West Texas accent. The day after I graduated from high school, I fled to the big city; in this case, it was Dallas. It was 1979, and I immediately got lost in the popular gay lifestyle of the day. It was very enticing for a boy fresh off the farm. I had my share of good times and bad. Today, I realize that much of my behavior during that period was extremely self-destructive. Unfortunately, I discovered that I had something new to hide. I had become infected with HIV, the virus that causes AIDS.

One day I found something that helped rescue me from my self-destructive course. What I discovered was an amazing church, a place where I belonged just as I was. Over the years, the love and acceptance I found there have given me the strength to face AIDS with hope and a healthier lifestyle. Learning to live with faith has always been a very slow process, but each day brought new lessons and new hope. Although I continued to experience the side effects of the virus and was forced to take disability because of my illness, I continued to practice faith until I had faith.

Today, I have gone from disability and a t-

cell count of 36 to a count of more than 300. My viral load is not detectable, and the best advice my doctor has been able to give me is to stop gaining weight and go back to work. I feel I have been given a second chance, and each day fills me with joy.

I know that the virus is not gone, but it is reasonable to expect that it is now a controllable disease that I can live with. The reward for my patience and perseverance is the newfound knowledge that I can make a difference in the world with God's help. Now the challenge is how to do that for the next 50 years or so.

Daryl symbolizes those extraordinary people who have taken the pain, grief and suffering of the curse of HIV and other life-threatening illnesses and made them redemptive. Their lives embody the spirit of Isaiah's "suffering servant" and the spirit of Jesus. The prophet Isaiah long ago spoke of a servant whose suffering would have a redemptive effect on the whole world. In the historic context, the nation of Israel was the suffering servant of whom the prophet spoke. Ultimately, the church came to believe that the writer was foretelling the kind of messiah Jesus came to be. Christ's suffering was healing for all humankind.

But he was wounded for our transgressions, bruised for our iniquities; upon him was the punishment that made us whole, and by his stripes we are healed.

Isaiah 53:5

How this could be is one of the mysteries of human redemption. Although the suffering of persons with AIDS is not cosmically redemptive, there are many gifts this epidemic will leave humankind. The price has been far too high, but millions of non-HIV infected people have been helped because of the medical breakthroughs that have resulted from AIDS. Through the suffering of our sisters and brothers has come healing and help that makes me know I am in the presence of the Holy with them.

In October of 1993, the Rev. Billy Graham apologized for having once said that AIDS was a divine judgment. He said he recognized that he did not really believe in a God like that and that what he had said was wrong. It was. AIDS is a virus, not an instrument of God. Sickle-cell anemia is not God's judgment on blacks. Breast cancer is not God's judgment on women, nor is Tay-Sachs disease God's judgment on Jewish children. In the United States, AIDS first infected the gay community, and, since it can be spread sexually, it has been spread largely within the gay community. If AIDS is a sign of God's displeasure at homosexuality in America, then God must not want Africans to be heterosexual, because it is that community that is dying of the disease on that continent. Accordingly, lesbians must be God's chosen people because they are among the least likely to contract AIDS.

The kind of theology that believes in a god of AIDS is sick. Men like Jerry Falwell and Pat Robertson, who heap guilt on the sick and dying, are the real evil that deserves to be quarantined from civilized society. Preachers like them have profaned the name of the God of Jesus Christ by their fixation with spreading their homo-hatred. Imagine for a moment the anguish they have caused for persons living with AIDS and for their families.

Our church adopted the following guiding statement in 1983:

> *We commit ourselves to be vigilant, outspoken opponents of any theology that even suggests that any disease is God's divine earthly retribution against any individual or group, and we resolve to*

*preach, teach and proclaim God's loving, healing
power and desire for our health and happiness.*

In the ninth chapter of the Gospel of John, there is
a story of a man who was born blind, whom Jesus healed.
When they came upon the man, the disciples asked Jesus,
"Rabbi, who sinned, this man or his parents, that he was
born blind?" (Like many modern disciples, they wanted
to talk theology in the face of this man's suffering.) Jesus
answered, "Neither, but his suffering is an opportunity for
God to be glorified." Although it is true that we reap what
we sow, there are bad things that happen to us, like what
happened to this man in the ninth chapter of John, that are
no one's fault. They can, however, be opportunities for good
to happen.

We live in a world estranged from God. We live in
a world filled with death and disease. Someday we will
find a cure for AIDS, and, along the way, we may discover
cures and treatments for a whole range of other diseases.
Our suffering may extend the life expectancy of the entire
human race. Out of our pain and suffering and death will
come healing and life for others. It is not a course any of
us would have chosen, but when our community has borne
this cross, like Jesus, we will offer the human race a great
gift, bought at a very high price.

Already, we are teaching communities to care for their
sick. Our church has mobilized hundreds of volunteers and
raised thousands of dollars to care for persons living with
AIDS. We adapted our care-teams to assist women with breast
cancer and people living with other life-threatening diseases.
All over this country, the lesbian and gay community has
worked tirelessly to help persons living with AIDS. These
are the real heroes of our day: the drag queens who have
raised hundreds of thousands of dollars; the sissy boys who
get squeamish at a hangnail but who have learned to clean

catheters and bed pans; the tough lesbians who have held their brothers, weeping while they died; the thousands of young men who have died with courage, never losing their dignity or sense of humor. They have taught us how to care for one another and reminded us what life really means.

One day I stopped by the hospital to make sure Jeff got his lunch. It was cold by the time I got there and did not look like it had much promise even when it was fresh. Still, he ate it as if it were a great feast.

I finally said, "Jeff, can I go get you some real food?"

"No, thank you," came his reply, "this is one of the best meals I ever tasted."

I guess I must have looked at him as if he had lost his mind because he explained, "You know pastor, ever since I was diagnosed, I have relished every meal I eat and every experience of my life. I'm just sorry it took finding out I was going to die to teach me what it means to live."

Jeff got sick before they learned to treat AIDS, so he died quickly. The day I conducted his memorial service, I could honestly say to his lover and family that he was a person who had discovered life. That is more than I could say at the funerals of some people who lived to be a hundred. This awful disease has taught us to care for one another, it has brought out the best in us, it has motivated us to get organized, and it has deepened our appreciation for life.

AIDS has come bearing another costly gift as well. It has brought a spiritual rebirth to the lesbian and gay community. Some of us have returned to the church for the first time to attend funerals of friends, and, there, we found a God of love that was unlike the gods of our childhood. Lesbian and gay people have always been deeply spiritual people, but now we are reclaiming the church from which we have too long been excluded.

In spite of all of the dreadful things that believers have done in the name of Christianity, Jesus is still the best and clearest revelation of God. We must not allow anyone to take that truth from us. We have to continue to confront homophobia within mainline denominations. At the same time, we must create our own spiritual communities that can tell the truth with power and persuasion. We, too, must take to the airwaves to tell the world that what it has heard for too long is a lie. We must speak the liberating truth to our sisters and brothers, and we must offer the truth to our heterosexual families and friends. We must preach, teach and embody the truth that lesbian and gay people can be happy, healthy and holy.

In the August 1992 issue of Qualitative Health Research, there was a touching story of a mother named Anne whose son Robert had become very sick with AIDS. Anne writes:

> *Five days before he died, his feet swelled a lot. They were always real, real swollen. He'd have to soak them in cold water. And we'd soak one first, then dry it off. Then the other. His feet were very tender. And so, you just had to be down on your knees and be very careful. I was down on my knees patting one foot dry and getting ready to soak the other one. Suddenly he looks down at me and says, "I trust you completely." And I said, "What?" And he repeated it. That meant more to me than all the "I love you's" in the world. I kept thinking, why does that mean so much, and I finally figured out . . . because that told me he knew how much I loved him. 'Cause, "I love you" is saying what I feel, but "I trust you completely" is saying, "I really do believe that you love me." And I did, so I really felt grateful.*

This mother learned about love at the feet of a son

with AIDS. What a tragedy that the Church of Jesus Christ has so missed the beautifully redemptive presence of God in the lives and deaths of those among us with AIDS. Mother Teresa said, "People living with AIDS are Jesus in a distressing disguise." Let us care for one another with the same tenderness and faithfulness that we would if we really believed Jesus when he said, "Whatever you do to the least, you do to me." Sometimes lesbian and gay people think that they are less loved and less accepted than straight folks. Maybe we should remember how closely Jesus identified with those who are the least.

I grew up in the Catholic Church and went to Catholic grade school and high school. I always enjoyed the structure of the services and feeling a part of something larger than my simple existence. However, it seems that I've spent my life searching for God and often falling short. I remember times when I felt lost and made my way back to a church in whatever city I lived in at the time, but never gaining a feeling of acceptance of finding the answers I was searching for.

My life has changed so much in the past few years. First and foremost, becoming a father has called me to a new place in my life and my faith. But for the first time, I feel like God has been searching for me, and I have felt his hand holding my heart. The Cathedral of Hope's most important lesson is "radical inclusion." In this hate-filled and discriminatory world we live in, I truly believe that God is smiling at the work he is doing through you and the pastors at CoH.

Ken Manford
Atlanta, GA

Chapter 12

Marry Me ...

On November 18, 2003, the Supreme Court of Massachusetts followed the model of our neighbors to the north in Canada and ruled that lesbian and gay citizens deserve the same rights as heterosexual citizens. Two months later, in his State of the Union address, George W. Bush called for a Constitutional Amendment to prevent other states from following Massachusetts' example.

With that, gay marriage became a "wedge issue" for politicians and a fundraising bonanza for the Religious Right. Above the din, which has provided more thunder than lightening, I have to remind our community of one basic principle:

*It is **not** about marriage. It is about discrimination.*

Let me explain. On December 12, 1912, U.S. Representative Seaborn Roddenberry of Georgia proposed a Constitutional Amendment that read in part:

Intermarriage between Negroes or persons of color and Caucasians within the United States ... is forever prohibited.

This amendment failed to pass, though 90 percent of Americans at the time opposed interracial marriage. By 1958 the opposition was up to 96 percent. That year, a Virginia judge explained that state's law barring interracial marriages by saying:

> *Obviously Almighty God did not intend for the*
> *races to mix since each race was initially placed on*
> *a separate continent.*

The U.S. Supreme Court finally overturned those laws, but that did not happen until 1967.

According to surveys conducted in 2005, about 60 percent of Americans oppose same-sex marriage. While it is unlikely that a federal Constitutional Amendment banning same-sex marriage will pass, we have seen many states pass their own Constitutional Amendments, which in some cases ban civil unions and could even prohibit domestic partner benefits.

It is probably not coincidental that the very states that were the last to give up racial marriage discrimination have been the first to pass laws excluding lesbian and gay people from marrying. Like all laws that institutionalize discrimination, the battle for marriage equality could do great harm to our community. The danger lies in our government making lesbian and gay people second-class citizens eligible for a whole range of discrimination.

This is not a battle we can win alone, however. The United States has a history of protecting minority rights and resisting discrimination, but we have seldom done so willingly, quickly or easily. For this reason, we need all the help we can get in the struggle for equality.

I believe that at least half of those who opinion polls say oppose same-sex marriage do so with very limited information or consideration. That is because most lesbian and gay people have not talked to their families and friends about this issue. If we remain silent then we are the ones to blame for their uninformed opinions.

We should probably be honest here. We are losing

this battle, in part, because our own community has great ambiguity about the issue of marriage. Marriage, in its present form, has rightly been seen as a flawed, and generally sexist, institution. Many of us do not want simply to buy into an institution that, historically, has been based more on property rights than on love.

In heterosexual marriages, for instance, the pastor traditionally asks, "Who **gives** this woman to be married to this man?" Women were historically regarded as property to be given and received. The idea behind a dowery was that a father **paid** a man to take his daughter off his hands. It is little wonder we want no part of **that** system.

Since the time of Ruth and Naomi and of David and Jonathan people of the same gender have made sacred covenants of love. So why do we need the state's approval of our relationships now?

The main issue is that, in this country, there are more than 1,100 civil protections afforded legally married couples that are not available to same-sex couples. Britney Spears, who got married for 24 **hours** as a joke, received all of those rights, yet gay and lesbian couples together for 24 **years** get none of them. Rights like:

- **Hospital Visitation:** Heterosexually married couples are considered next-of-kin for hospital visitation and in making medical decisions. I have seen long-term partners excluded from their dying lovers' hospital rooms because they were not legally family.
- **Ultimate Decisions:** The legal protection of marriage is the only way to ensure we get to make ultimate decisions for our loved ones upon their death.

As an example, one member of this congregation, who died of AIDS many years ago, had been very specific about his desire to be cremated and to have his ashes interred in the Memorial Garden of this church. He did not want to be buried in his hometown, which had been abusive to him when he was young. He wrote out his wishes and made his partner promise to carry them out.

Upon his death, however, his biological family swooped in, took possession of everything in the home, which the couple jointly owned, and claimed the body.

When I contacted an attorney on behalf of the partner, I was informed that, in Texas, dead people have no rights and that the next-of-kin gets to make all of the decisions. Before we could get a hearing in court the grieving partner had lost everything they owned in addition to the love of his life.

- **Social Security Benefits**: Married couples receive Social Security payments upon the death of a spouse. Despite paying the **same taxes**, however, lesbian and gay couples do not receive a penny, regardless of how many years they were together.

- **Immigration**: Our church is often called upon to help couples where one partner is in danger of being deported because they are not a U.S. citizen. A heterosexual, non-U.S. citizen can meet someone in a bar, marry the next day and then be allowed to stay in this country, while long-term same-gender couples are forced to split up or move to another country.

- **Health Insurance:** Many corporate and government employees are able to provide health insurance to their husbands and wives, but same-gender couples don't receive this benefit. Even if a company does provide domestic partner benefits, the same-gender partner is forced to pay income tax on the value of the insurance.

- **Estate Taxes:** A married person automatically inherits all the property belonging to his or her spouse without paying taxes. A gay or lesbian spouse must go through the probate process to retain even their own home. If the estate is great enough, the surviving partner must pay estate taxes as if they had received an inheritance from a stranger.

- **Retirement Savings:** A married person can roll a deceased spouse's 401k funds into an IRA without paying taxes, but a lesbian or gay American who inherits their partner's 401K will end up paying a tax liability that can be as great as 70 percent of the money they spent their lives together saving.
- **Family Leave**: Married workers are legally entitled to unpaid leave from their jobs to care for an ill spouse. Gay and lesbian workers have no such rights. During the AIDS crisis many gay men had to chose between losing their jobs and abandoning their dying partners.
- **Nursing Homes**: Although none of us believe it will ever come to this for us, it will. Married couples have a legal right to live out their last days together in a nursing home. Lesbian and gay couples have no such protection at the end of their lives.
- **Home Protection**: Laws protect married seniors from being forced to sell their homes to pay for the cost of their partner's nursing home care. Same-gender couples have no such protection. If you jointly own the home, you can be forced to sell it and give the nursing home half or, if you are able, buy back half of your own home from your spouse.
- **Pensions:** After the death of an employee, most pension plans pay survivor benefits, but they will only pay a legally married spouse. A gay or lesbian partner of a lifelong employee is left with nothing.

This list could go on, but I hope you see that this is an

issue with significant implications. I remind you that these are **civil rights** that are being denied to **American taxpayers**. Regardless of how someone might feel about the religious issues surrounding marriage, this is not about marriage; it is about **discrimination.**

In the 1970s there was a great poster that hung in many churches that said, "Ordain women or stop baptizing them!" The point, of course, was that there are no second-class Christians. Well, there ought not to be second-class citizens either, so I am proposing this poster:

Marry gay people or stop taxing them.

The truth that I keep trying to communicate to people is simply this: The Cathedral of Hope has been marrying same-gender couples since 1970. The United Church of Christ, Unitarian Universalists and Metropolitan Community Churches also marry same-gender couples, as do others. I have personally married hundreds of couples. No one has died, civilization has not come to an end, and the institution of marriage has not been harmed in any way that can be traced to those services.

The Cathedral of Hope marries both heterosexual couples and homosexual couples. We use the same ritual, exchange the same rings, say the same vows. In fact, the **only** difference between the two services is that heterosexual couples walk out of church with more than 1,100 civil rights and protections that the same-sex taxpayers don't get.

That is discrimination, and it has *nothing* to do with what the Bible says and doesn't say about marriage. It has nothing to do with religion; churches have always been free to do these services or not. Many churches will not remarry divorced people. While I disagree with that position, it is interesting that Jesus actually talked about divorce and remarriage, but he never talked about homosexuality.

Ironically, divorce is one of the many marriage issues about which our culture has made dramatic shifts in the not too distant past. Religious institutions resisted that shift for some time, but the overwhelming majority of churches has been able to adapt to a more graceful way.

Marriage is a civil right that is often, but not necessarily, blessed by a religious ceremony. It is not a religious ceremony authorized by the state. Even when I perform heterosexual marriages I never say the words, "By the power vested in me by the State of Texas, I now pronounce you ..." As a pastor, I am clear that any power of authority I have comes from God, not from the state. I can preside over a couple making sacred covenants before family and friends. The government bestows or withholds the civil rights and protections afforded married couples, and it is discrimination to grant those rights to certain taxpayers and withhold them from others. Same-gender marriage is not a religious issue, but while we are on that subject, there are some things we should note.

"Leadership Journal" is a fairly fundamentalist Christian publication. In an issue published after the Massachusetts Supreme Court ruling that led to that state legalizing same-sex marriage, they interviewed four evangelical pastors about the issue. Tony Campolo, whom I love, had this to say when the interviewer asked, "So the biblical model of marriage is one man, one woman, one lifetime?"

> A "biblical model" is harder to establish than you think. A colleague of mine has identified, I think, 16 models of marriage in the Hebrew Bible, including polygamy, concubinage, handmaidens, levirate arrangements, purchasing of wives, and spouses that accompany political alliances. It's so pious to say "the biblical model of marriage." Which of those forms of marriage do you mean?

John Yates, an Episcopal priest in Virginia and friend of President Bush, said:

> *I believe Genesis 2 gives us the foundation—a man and woman leaving, cleaving, and becoming one flesh—and then I jump to Mark 10 and Jesus' understanding of the permanence of that relationship.*

To this, Campolo said:

> *Speaking of Mark 10, what do you do with divorced people who remarry? Do you accept them in church? I mean, while Jesus never speaks about gay marriage, he speaks very clearly about those who remarry after a divorce. I don't know many churches that enforce a no-remarriage rule. Has the church said, "We have to be faithful to Scripture about marriage, except on the issue of divorce and remarriage?" Or do we extend grace? Because if we're going to show grace toward people who are divorced and remarried, an area Jesus specifically called sin, then how do you **not** show grace to people in a sexual relationship that Jesus never mentions?*

Well, there you have it right from the mouth of one of America's most prominent evangelicals. It is remarkable how, in the past 50 years, the church has dramatically shifted its stand on divorce. Some of us are old enough to remember when divorced persons were not allowed to serve in leadership in churches and were disqualified from ordination.

Over the past few decades, though, we have been guided by grace and reinterpreted the teachings of Jesus in our modern context. Yet when it comes to a topic about which Jesus said **NOTHING**, most churches remain legalistic, punitive and primitive in their thinking.

In our conversations with family and friends, it might be helpful to raise the issue of what Jesus said about divorce:

> *And I say to you, whoever divorces his wife, except for unchastity, and marries another commits adultery.*
>
> Matthew 19:9

Except for the most legalistic and fundamentalist, few Americans believe that divorce, while unfortunate, is actually sinful. Divorced heterosexuals are not treated as sinners, though these words appear in red in the gospels.

Churches interpret these words because the world is different from the one in which Jesus spoke. That is how it should be, but why is that different from same-sex couples asking for civil rights for their relationships? The whole issue of same-gender marriage is about justice and fairness, but what you so often get are irrational arguments like:

Q: Isn't marriage really for procreation?

A: *Does that mean older people beyond childbearing age shouldn't be allowed to marry?*

Q: So where does it stop? Why not allow polygamy?

A: *If polygamous marriages were allowed for heterosexuals then they should be allowed for homosexuals. Until then, this is beside the point.*

Q: What's wrong with civil unions? Do you have to call it marriage?

A: *During the civil rights movement we learned what was wrong with "separate but equal." It is rarely equal. In this case, you can have a civil union in Vermont, but it is meaningless in Texas. Civil unions don't address the hundreds of federal rights being denied same-sex taxpayers.*

In talking to our family and friends, I think there are two keys to being successful. First, we should listen to their concerns. If we can, provide additional facts and information that are helpful. Ultimately, though, it is difficult to argue with an irrational fear.

In the end, what is most critical is for you to tell them your own story. They need to hear why this matters to you, how it makes you feel to be treated like a second-class citizen and human. Your story is something no one can argue with. In the end, we are counting on a verse from the Bible being true. I John 4:18 says:

Perfect love casts out all fear.

We are counting on the love of the people who know you to overcome their irrational fear of change. Ultimately, we serve a God who said:

Behold, I make all things new.
Revelation 21:5

Who knows? Perhaps if we live with faith rather than fear, that same God may make the whole institution of marriage new, by making us all, gay and straight alike, take it more seriously and understand what it really means.

I think the thing that makes a journey to Christ so personal and powerful at Cathedral of Hope is the fact that many of us venture into an honest relationship with God at approximately the same time we venture into an honest relationship with ourselves. Throughout my married life, I think I knew there was something different about me, and being the overachiever that I am, I got heavily involved in my Methodist church. Even before I came out, I came to CoH in the middle of the week, "just to look around." I couldn't let anyone see me there, but I HAD to see what was inside the building. I was awestruck at the beauty and quietness of the sanctuary with no one there. I realized that SOMEDAY I needed to actually attend church there. But how?

That was soon resolved with my coming out and leaving my wife of 16 years. I visited on a Sunday morning, and again had the same concerns about "being seen." However, the sermon was so powerful, and the music so incredibly uplifting and engaging, that I spent most of the service with tears in my eyes. I have been a Christian all my life and never really had this sort of emotional interaction with (and especially IN) my church. I finally felt like I belonged, for the first time in my life. I found myself becoming bolder and more confident in debating people who claim homosexuality is a sin. I found that some of the people that I thought would never understand actually did, and I've become closer to them than ever before. I began to see that people who were not like me worshiped the same God I do, and, for the first time in my life, I knew that God really was important to everybody, not just to me.

Jacque Borel
Dallas, Texas

Appendix

A Psychiatrist Talks about Homosexuality

James C. "Jes" Montgomery, M.D. has been a psychiatrist in private practice in Dallas, Texas since 1995. Prior to training in psychiatry, he practiced family medicine and addiction medicine in Lafayette, Louisiana. Born in Lafayette, Dr. Montgomery first considered a career in the Methodist ministry, working with youth groups and church choirs until college graduation in 1976. He graduated medical school from Louisiana State University Medical Center in New Orleans in December 1979 and completed a family practice residency in 1982. When the oil industry hit its low in the mid 1980s, the change in his family medicine practice led him to work in addiction medicine and, later, psychiatry. He was, for five years, the medical director of the Pride Program, a nationally-owned program for treating lesbians, gays, and bisexual and transgender people in need of treatment for chemical dependency or psychiatric care. As a member of the Board of Directors of the Society for the Advancement of Sexual Health (SASH), he was able to join with others to speak for the LGBT community in the area of sexual addiction, and has spoken numerous times on topics related to lesbian and gay issues at the American Society on Addiction Medicine, SASH, Gay and Lesbian Medical Association, and other educational settings. In addition, he has served on the board of directors of the Resource Center of Dallas. Outside his career, he enjoys life as a partner, a father of three, and a grandfather of four. A member of the Cathedral of Hope since 1998, Dr. Montgomery graciously offers, as a person of faith, some of the insights he has gained through years working with, and among, the lesbian, gay, bisexual and transgender community.

Let me begin by simply saying this: HOMOSEXUALITY (along with lesbianism, bisexuality, transexuality and intersexism) IS NOT, I REPEAT, NOT A PSYCHIATRIC ILLNESS. As I write, I realize that the committees that will write the Diagnostic and Statistical Manual (DSM-V)[1] are being formed and the fireworks will begin in every area of psychiatric diagnosis. However, for decades, the mere attraction to something other than a member of the opposite sex generally has been accepted to be no indicator of psychopathology, our word for psychiatric or psychological illness.

In spite of this, every year, the syllabus for the American Psychiatric Association (APA) general meeting contains at least one presentation by the stalwarts of "reparative therapy" and other means to "treat" homosexuality—a genre of therapy for a disease that is accepted not to exist. What is even more humorous to me is that the Association of Gay and Lesbian Psychiatrists (AGLP) is probably the single largest block group within the APA. No other faction can mobilize more than a thousand votes on any item in the larger organization within minutes. When the AGLP gets together, anybody who is anybody, or wants to be anybody, in the APA shows up to shake hands and rub elbows.

Having said that, I also will say that growing up lesbian, gay, bisexual or transgender will drive anyone crazy! The gay youth is asked to navigate through life without a compass, map or guide. At the same time, he or she is held to a standard that is far higher than that of any peer. My firm belief is that growing up gay IS a chronic, constant and repetitive trauma and leaves the gay adult with all the subtle symptoms of Post Traumatic Stress Disorder (PTSD). Those symptoms include avoidance of situations that remind one of the trauma (like family gatherings, churches, schools and work), startling easily, having recurrent intrusive thoughts and nightmares about the "trauma" (as is portrayed over and over in movies about being gay), and hyper-vigilance (always being on guard).

My first true glimpse into this hyper-vigilance came at Logan Airport in Boston, on September 25, 2001. Within days of the tragedy of 9/11, the airport was barely a ghost town, with perhaps 100 passengers in the entire terminal and huge planes flying with less than one-third of their seats full. Standing at the juncture of the concourses, the group with which I was traveling chatted before our flight. We were an unseemly bunch: a mixture of all sexual orientations containing two psychiatrists, two therapists, two spouses and two normal people. Leave it to one of the psychiatrists to point to the security area and challenge us to identify who was gay and who was not. Because the stream of people was so sparse and so steady, the task was straightforward. (Though we certainly could not rely on the stereotypes that Hollywood usually offers!)

We quickly identified a process that is still applicable today. The extremely frequent travelers (traumatized by that frequent traveler), those in the military, those who probably had overt trauma, and the LGBT people always go through the scanner on the first pass. They have their belts and shoes off, their IDs and their boarding passes in their hands and rarely, if ever, have to go back through the scanner, never having to be hand scanned (unless the "jewelry" is 0 gauge or larger!).

When one has spent the majority of life scanning every situation to see how to act, how to talk, who is safe, who may understand, who responds to what comment in what manner, and who notices what glance, the process of going through level "Super Purple Red" at security is a cinch! Think about it: What was it like, before puberty set in, trying to figure out what that warm feeling was about and why it happened with this girl or boy and not with that boy or girl? What happened when you realized you were the only one in junior high P.E. that actually WANTED to take showers?!? What was it like in high school to note where the gay bar was in town, not because you wanted to know what the jokes were about, but because you really wanted to know where it was? Then, there were the drives-by, scanning to make sure nobody saw that you actually were looking to see it ... each of the six times you drove by! I could continue through life, but won't.

However, I do have to visit the family. What was it like to realize that you were the only one in the family that understood those nuances other family members missed and said, "I don't get it" about? Like when something "gay" came on the news or, goddess forbid, in the family. What does it do to a teen to hear his or her father say, as I've heard patients describe at least twice, "Matthew Shepard wouldn't have to worry about no gay-bashers. I'd have put a bullet in his head long before that and put him out of his misery"? In my opinion, prisoners may be treated better than LGBT youth and young adults. At least they KNOW they are in prison.

Given this, is it any wonder that the assumption is that "normal" for LGBT persons is neurotic and at least "a half a bubble off level?" Add to that foundation the additional trauma that coming out brings, such as being rejected by family and friends, social isolation and gay-bashing. Regardless, let me reiterate: HOMOSEXUALITY (even in the face of this foundation) IS NOT A PSYCHIATRIC DISEASE.

Part of what a healthy psyche needs in youth is a set of firm boundaries to challenge. I think I can count my children as reasonably healthy (at least within the two standard deviations of the mean on the bell curve!). Each of them had times when I thought they were going to go over the edge and take off on some kind of weird or lost tangent. I wish they had always followed the paths I would have set out for them. Yet, they needed to find out who they are. On top of that, they had the right to make the mistakes they needed to make. Unfortunately, they have chosen to make some of the same mistakes that I made and that I warned them about. (Go figure!) They found their parents to be stupid, just like I did! However, I do believe that what they, like all developing psyches, needed were some bottom lines. They needed to know that, if required, one of their parents would turn into some sort of monster that would drag them out of the swampy mess they had created. What they did NOT need was judgment, non-acceptance, rejection or a challenge to do it "my way, or else."

If any of us remember adolescence, we recall how dumb our parents were and how frequently we did the opposite of what they told us. When a youth is struggling with difficult issues and a parent presents them with rigid, unfeeling attitudes that imply the lack of acceptance, the youth is essentially forced to go underground and do the opposite. This obligatory secrecy becomes the stealth that gives the LGBT youth the emotional trauma that parallels covert military trainees.

A secondary part of this developmental trauma is that LGBT youth do not have an "age appropriate" area in which to explore developing sexuality. While those of us who have made it into the circles may joke about the "lizards and chicken hawks"[2] in the bars, where else do the youth have to go to explore being gay? Even stepping into a LGBT youth center becomes a potential "scarlet letter" for the "questioning" youth. Once he or she steps into those unhallowed halls, the secret is out, and the label may well be applied permanently. "Guess who's gay!" becomes the underground headline. Suddenly, a scared young person has all sorts of stares and unsolicited "friends" that publicly identify them as having resolved their ambivalence. For some reason, the LGBT community seems to have an aversion to allowing closet doors to have hinges. Those doors need to be dynamited off!

The reality is that most pre-teen and teenaged gays learn what they learn by blind experimentation (usually done in full blown denial), non-age appropriate experimentation (usually with an abusive age-based power differential), or by stepping into the "adult" gay world. We all know how careful the backdoor checkers at gay bars can be, especially in small towns or at out-of-the-way bars. Somehow, if the diaper is off and the shoes are tied, someone will help the young LGBT person onto the bar stool. Intentionally or not, the gay bar scene becomes the "library" of information for young people to "study" being gay.

In reality, a terrified, socially unprepared teenager (regardless of what the chronological age is) steps into a dark, loud, clandestine world, electrified with sexual energy. To be the center of attention, to receive looks and touch that were once but a fantasy, and even to be partially accepted can shatter even the healthiest judgment. In the façade of "freedom," the possibilities become myriad, and the truth of ignorance—what we don't know can't possibly hurt us, can it?—sweeps a wide-eyed young person to heights untold. Add a bit of alcohol, a touch of drugs and sexual arousal, and a life may be changed forever. THIS is the TRUE gay life, isn't it?

I certainly hope not. Yet, where is a questioning young person to learn anything different? The bars and the bathhouses are easy to find. Gyms, adult bookstores and cruise areas are virtually ubiquitous. Large cities have their "gayborhoods." Yet, are any of these actually the places one would want to take or send a LGBT adolescent to learn about being gay, like we send youth to 4-H to learn leadership skills? Is it any surprise that the lessons learned are so very skewed and distorted? Growing up gay WILL drive you CRAZY!

Finding Mental Health in a Crazy World

Having defined the world of growing up gay as crazy-making, what is a poor lesbian, gay, bisexual or transgender person to do? My first hint would be to find a home! By that, I mean a place that feels like the place you want to go no matter how you feel. I'd highly recommend a place that uses terms such as "inclusive," "regardless" and "accepting." One of the major things that happens when we grow up in the mine field of uncertainty is that we feel the loss of "community," the loss of a sense of true "family." I always have found it a paradoxically prophetic truth that LGBT people frequently refer to each other as "family." (Often with an apparent extra "a," as in "fa-amily!"). I think this speaks to a true need for a deeper sense of connection. This is one of the roles the Church can, and must, fulfill if the homosexual community is to break free of its own stereotypes and cycles of trauma and fear. We all need to be connected on the spiritual and social levels, even more than on the physical level.

One of Maslow's most basic needs in the "Hierarchy of Needs"[3] is a sense of belonging and feeling loved. For Maslow, this need comes after physiologic and survival needs (food and water) and a sense of safety. The sense of belonging to a community or family, and of being loved and lovable, grows out of a sense of being able to protect ourselves, and is based on the sense of safety. Young children appear to love being startled and tossed into the air, seeming to seek danger. In reality, what they crave is the safety that comes in being held while being startled and being caught safely after flying through the air. Children instinctively seem to trust their parents explicitly and implicitly. When they are caught and safely startled in "peek-a-boo" in the arms of adults, they learn to feel safe within themselves.

Maslow's Hierarchy of Needs.
Taken from "Motivation and Personality"

When we grow up feeling as though we are "different" and have no frame of reference for understanding our sense of self, the need for a sense of connection becomes deeper and stronger, especially if any hope of developing a sense of what Maslow called "self-actualization" or self knowledge. By the time a young LGBT person has an opportunity to actually step into a "real" gay community, the desperate need for some sense of belonging has become a black hole that may well reach into their soul. Many have no foundation on which to base their sense of self.

If they have been the recipient of abuse by a member of the same sex, many questions they have about bodies and sex may be answered, while adding tons of confusion through shattered boundaries. To add shame to chaos and confusion, the innocent young person who already feels defective and "queer" receives the covert message—one that never has to be spoken—that he or she "deserved" that abuse. Let me affirm loudly: NOBODY EVER, EVER DESERVES TO BE ABUSED. That means being touched, sexualized or used for sex without their consent. However, when a child or young person is questioning his or her own worth or value because of feelings that are socially unacceptable, and an older, larger or more experienced person imposes their power on them, consent is impossible. Little Red Riding Hood cannot give consent to the Big Bad Wolf, ever. I could write an entire book about this aspect of growing up gay, but simply will repeat once more that ABUSE IS NEVER THE VICTIM'S FAULT. A more important impact is that the victimized young person mistakes his or her curiosity for fault or blame. Nothing could be farther from the truth!

Even if a gay youth escapes without overt trauma, the journey to knowing a sense of self and establishing connections with others is still not an easy one. Without a map or a compass, the journey through the mine field of society, religion, family and friends continues to be saturated with challenges, fear and confusion.

The journey out of "the closet," or the isolation of uncertainty, into identity is one that is never finished alone. Every human being is genetically a composite of generations of DNA. Each and every human psyche is the accumulation of all we inherit, all we learn, all we see and all we fantasize. Whether we are aware that we take in these messages or not, who we are is based on what we absorb, reject and react to from those around us. Many gay people have ended up with bitter, distorted views of themselves and the LGBT community because of the distortion that isolation and loneliness create. They are trying to heal wounds made during developing years. To do this is difficult without love and support. To feel as though the only "community" or source of belonging comes in the dimly lit world of the clandestine can only lend a deep sense of futility. This is one area where the church can and must reach out. An accepting and affirming spiritual environment is one of the few places where a young LGBT person can stand up in the light of day, with head held high, and feel the embrace of community.

One of the greatest gifts of the Cathedral of Hope is the fact that it is such a large collection of people. The overwhelming majority of these people are very clear about who they are, have esteem for themselves, and clearly feel that they belong. I have watched many relatively predictable responses from people visiting the Cathedral for the first time. Inevitably, the fear and disbelief follow them well into the service. However, it is difficult to avoid being swept into the warmth and energy of the worship. Many times, the mark of the newcomer is the notable, if not open, weeping that happens after communion. For many, this is the first time in their conscious lives that they have actually heard and felt the message that they belong. For some, it is a reconnection with a spiritual path they believed they lost when they found themselves. It is the first opportunity to receive a sacrament that they believed was no longer open to them.

Many may prefer a smaller venue, and I certainly encourage seeking that, if that is your preference. The Dallas-Fort Worth Metroplex is not that different from many major cities. It has numerous churches, and at least one synagogue, that declare themselves primarily gay and lesbian houses of worship. Many other mainstream denominations provide "open and affirming" congregations. The key thing is that the place of worship provides a sense of community.

I'm Not Crazy, What Do You Mean Mental Health?

Okay, so I'm beginning to sound like the kind of psychiatrist that Hollywood loves to portray, saying one thing and then saying the opposite. Let me review. I am working on the assumption that growing up lesbian, gay, bisexual or transgender one misses out on the full development of a sense of belonging and a sense of safety that are necessary to develop a sense of self and a sense of self-esteem, which are Maslow's primary needs beyond the essentials of food and water. I do not believe that any of us goes through this gauntlet without some wounds and without needing some healing. Being LGBT means facing life on different terms. This means carrying some wounds and facing some losses. The shame and fear that are attached to asking for help with healing that does not involve a physical, visible wound in our culture deepens this shame. We seem to live under the notion that if it's not something you can see measured in the body then the problem must be "in your head." What this really ends up meaning is that the problem doesn't exist. When we talk about a "problem" that is hidden, secret or brings about social scorn and contempt, that existence is even less likely.

What about Mental Health in an Unhealthy World?

Unfortunately, many young people have turned to the mental health community to seek a sense of acceptance and community. I cringe when I hear stories about people whose parents promptly hauled them to a psychiatrist after the young person came out. I must admit that I loudly applaud those mental health providers who listened intently, carefully assessed the young person realistically, and then told them that they were not psychiatrically sick and just needed to move forward. Unfortunately, I still fear that these clinicians are in the minority. I must admit that I've not always navigated these rocky waters as well as I would have liked and have probably made every mistake to which I wish I didn't have to admit. Trust me, "diversity" and "sensitivity" were not common in much of my training! Many times, when a family engages the mental health system, they do not want to hear that no "cure" exists, so they leave angry. Some young people (of all ages) take my lack of "diagnosis" as the freedom to continue with stereotypical wild abandon and the proof that they can do whatever they want. Some are gracious, smiling and nodding to what I have to say, and then never return, retreating into their secret lives. Unfortunately, most are still afraid to come out of the true veil of secrecy that remains within them.

Not everybody needs therapy, but many need some guidance. How DO you pick a mental health guide through rough waters? This is not an easy question to answer. I'll just list some of the things that I've had to debate repeatedly over the years, along with my thoughts:

- **Does a metal health provider NEED to be lesbian, gay, bisexual or transgender to be effective?** Not absolutely. Many people, both professional and in the LGBT community, feel that being gay biases the therapy and clouds the objectivity of the therapist. Likewise, being "too heterosexual" leaves a therapist without an understanding of the language and nuances of LGBT culture, which, in reality, also creates a bias and clouds the therapy. A key issue then becomes internalized homophobia, which, by the way, most LGBT people do not believe they have and will spend a lot of time arguing about. If the therapist is too close to any stereotype, positive or negative, the client or patient will be forced to either idealize the therapist or sabotage the therapy.

In the end, the only issue that really matters is that the person seeking the therapy feels comfortable and challenged at the same time. A therapist who always gives good news and never challenges is a salesperson, not a therapist. One who is always in conflict with the one seeking therapy has, in all likelihood, become one of the client's parents in disguise. Either way, growth cannot occur.

- **Does the provider have to know everything about being LGBT to be effective?** That would be impossible. This is a very diverse community. However, I do not expect my patients to teach me. If someone seeking therapy spends as much time educating the therapist as getting therapy, then the therapy is not going to be as effective as it could be. Every day, I am challenged to learn something new. If I really do my job, my patients never know how much I have to learn and they do NOT have to teach me.

- **Do I have to be subtle with a therapist?** Nope. One thing I've had to learn in working with this community is that I had to get over being surprised long ago. I may be caught off guard a bit every now and then, but I haven't been shocked in years. In fact, I tend to do the opposite. My questions about safer sex to a newly out young person are rather blunt and specific. They usually tell me they know all about it, but I can teach them more in three minutes than they thought they wanted to know!

  That said, if a patient is out to surprise or shock me, a lot of time is going to be wasted in therapy. Sometimes, testing has to occur to establish trust. However, beyond the basic testing of trustworthiness, shock value has no place in therapy. On the other hand, if a therapist can't say "penis," "vagina," "vulva," "anal," "oral" and a few other common words about what people do in the process of relatively routine sexual exploration and behavior, then dealing with something outside heterosexual, male-superior, missionary-position sex on Friday with the lights out after the kids are in bed is going to be tough.

- **How long does it take to know if I can work with a therapist?** First of all, trust your gut. Our true intuition is rarely wrong. The problem is that we have to assess our intuition with our head. Second, give it a chance. Few of us wrote in our eighth-grade essay that we wanted to grow up and be in therapy about whether or not we should come out or face any of the issues that come with being LGBT. It's never very comfortable. I usually ask people to give me three tries to see if I make the cut. I also ask them to stick with it for up to 12 sessions and then re-assess. Finally, therapy should be going somewhere. What are YOUR goals, and what are the therapist's goals? Do they match? Are they changing to meet your needs? Ask to take a look at the theoretical "map" every now and then.

- **Can't I just take medicine and get over this? OR do I have to take "drugs" to deal with this?** I always tell people that medication in psychiatry is like tuning the engine on a car. The finest Ferrari may have a perfectly tuned engine, but it will be a miserable vehicle with two flat tires and a hole in the roof. Therapy changes the tires, and time patches the hole in the roof. Medication works slowly. (Rapid in psychiatry is 10 to 14 days!)

    The down side of this reality is that some of the symptoms that psychiatrists (and therapists) treat take time to get better. Unfortunately, we do not have a "pain reliever" or "aspirin" for some of these hurts. The treatments we do have may take days to be truly effective. That is why it is important for the provider to make an accurate diagnosis and for the patient to understand it. Medication is based on accurate diagnoses, not necessarily to treat symptoms. Depression is a serious, life-threatening illness. Panic is immobilizing anxiety. Mania may sound like fun, but it is devastating. Sometimes the symptoms overlap, and medication for one diagnosis makes another worse. When we're talking about something that will take days to significantly change, the correct diagnosis is essential and doesn't happen in five minutes.

The most sensitive (yet non-specific) indicators of psychiatric illness are changes in sleep or appetite, irritability or changes in temper, changes in concentration, or changes in energy—any of which is to the magnitude that it interferes with our interactions with others or our work. Unfortunately, these are the psychiatric equivalent of fever to the body. They point us in the direction of poor mental health, but in no way tell us what is going on.

Medication in psychiatry is an inexact science. What works for one person may fail miserably for another. What has horrible side effects for one person may be like taking water to another. What works beautifully for months may stop working under stress or change. Starting medication begins a whole new level of essential communication.

- **What is the end result of therapy?** I think a paraphrase of Freud's thoughts says it best: The goal of therapy is to be able to love, work and enjoy life the majority of days. However, these are broad, sweeping and general descriptions and may not really answer the question.

Much of the answer lies in the goals set for

the therapy. If I want to change a behavior, whether it is an outward behavior or an unpleasant inward reaction to family, friends, society or others, then, the end result is to be able to measure a change in that behavior. If the goal is to cope with stress differently, then managing a stressful situation is the end result. In the end, therapy is what a patient and a therapist design it to be. Nothing more and nothing less.

- **How do I know if I need therapy?** First of all, ask yourself if you can agree with Henry David Thoreau: "If the day and the night are such that you greet them with joy that is your success." If the answer is positive, you may not need therapy. If you're not sure, keep thinking.

   Next, ask if there are any patterns in your life that you don't like, don't like to talk about, or keep hidden. If there are—whether they are related to sex and sexuality or not—an objective guide may be very useful. If you have a behavior that you want to stop but can't seem to, or a behavior that you can't seem to control, whether it is chemically related or not, at least explore whether or not it's a problem.

   If going some place, seeing someone, talking about some topic, or encountering any other situation in life changes your mood dramatically that indicates a deep wound that is not healing well.

There are no right or wrong answers in taking care of yourself. The most important thing is being able to feel as though you are moving in the direction you want to be headed. Surround yourself with people you trust and ask them what they see as you move forward on your journey.

The Losses and Grief of Being LGBT

One of the things I think our society has an extremely difficult time with is the process of grief. We give it a lot of lip service but, in the end, avoid talking about how much grief and loss is involved in day-to-day life. We politically correct it as "empty nest syndrome" or a "midlife crisis" in order to avoid actually feeling the losses. We call these the "normal losses" in life and pretend they don't exist. For the person facing gay life, loss is a very real thing and one that must actively be addressed.

When I talk about grief, I mean the active process of facing the loss, having our soul touched by it and moving on into what Elizabeth Kubler-Ross called "acceptance"[4] and is sometimes also referred to as "saddened acceptance." We cannot change the losses. We have to face them and see how they have impacted us.

I finally got a true understanding of grief when I was escorted onto the Rio Grande Gorge Bridge outside Arroyo Hondo, New Mexico by my friend Rev. Ted Wiard, the founder of Golden Willow Retreat, a place for healing grief. Let me preface this by saying that I am deathly afraid of heights. Ted took me walking onto a bridge over a 590-foot gorge at 6:00 in the morning, which was not what I would have planned. Fortunately, I was given no option, all in good spirit. Standing on this magnificent bridge, I could see how a tectonic plate shift (literally a split in the flat surface of the earth) had basically created a HUGE rift, over which I was suspended. It is nearly a quarter of a mile across and, as I said, almost 600 feet down to where I could barely see the water. As I stood on the lookout in the middle of this bridge (albeit clutching the railing for dear life), I could hear the wind and feel the enormity of what was before me. I could experience with all my senses precisely what grief was: Something enormous was not where it should be. I have no concept of what power and force it would take to move the earth apart and create a gorge of this magnificent size and beauty. Yet, there I stood, mesmerized in the middle of it. I had been taken to a place that actually showed me what grief does in our lives. Grief suspends us over a huge gorge in what was supposed to be the solid ground of life.

From less than half a mile away, you cannot see the Rio Grande Gorge coming, much like the losses we discover in our lives. While Ted had shown me a video of the bridge and the gorge, I had no idea as we drove toward it what I was about to embrace. No matter how we prepare for losses or think we have "handled them," when we truly stand in the gap of a deep loss, we cannot fully be prepared for it. Our culture would have us simply turn away and keep marching as though nothing happened. In reality, when we know we have lost, we need to stand on that observation deck, clutch the safety rail and allow ourselves to be awestruck.

At some point in life, every LGBT person must face some degree of grief about the losses that come with being gay. Hopefully they are relatively insignificant. Yet, if they go unnoticed, they tend to grow and become stumbling blocks. I must emphasize that the goal is not any specific process, but acceptance that something has gone and cannot be recaptured. Here is a partial list of things to think about having lost:

- An adolescence filled with innocence and free exploration, replete with clumsiness, embarrassment and humor.
- The excitement of telling your parents how wonderful your real first love was and having them understand.
- Being able to talk to your same-sex parent about your feelings and get neutral, open feedback.
- Being able to find out if kissing a boy (or girl) really

was different from kissing a girl (or boy).

- Having a wedding, OR knowing that your wedding vows really meant what they said.
- NOT having a divorce.
- Having children, OR having children that weren't uncomfortable with who you are.
- Coming out without fear, OR knowing that coming out wasn't as bad as you thought (or was worse than you imagined).
- Growing old without fear of being labeled, lost or alone.
- Having a place to grow old.
- Having insurance benefits.
- Being able to tell people at work you are not single.
- Having any hope whatsoever of being CEO of a major corporation, even though you are "out."
- Being able to have sex with your partner without a condom or dental dam.
- Being able to go to your 20-year high school reunion or, if you go, being able to tell the truth and not that story you rehearsed all the way there.
- NOT being the only one at your 20-year high school reunion whose partner died.
- Being able to attend a party and bring the person with whom you share your life without fear of reprisal.
- Realizing that you didn't face the music and bring that person to all those parties.

In addition, other losses have to do with the wounds that come from the processes I've been talking about. Think about some of these:

- The irreparable change in your relationship with your parents when they first rejected you, even if you reconciled.

- The reality that our family of origin or biology—the people who were our primary caregivers—are not a part of our lives.
- Another birthday or holiday without a card from siblings or cousins that you saw every day through years of grade and high school.
- The promotions you doubt you'll ever get because they "know."
- The way you still notice how people look at you and your partner in the store, even after all these years.
- The friends you lost because, once you came out, you just didn't ever call them.
- The time wasted in a life you didn't want, longing for the one you didn't have.

The list goes on. In their book *Coming Out Within*,[5] Craig O'Neil and Kathleen Ritter touch on many of these subjects. While a morbid preoccupation with these losses is totally useless, my belief is that when these issues are not grieved, they become the framework for internalized homophobia, that deep anger the LGBT person carries towards self, most often projected onto other members of the community. Much like racism, the unfortunate truth is that the greatest source of homophobia lies within the community itself. I think the main source of this anger is the unresolved grief about these subtle losses and the wounds that go with them. In articles in the Journal of Gay and Lesbian Psychotherapy in 1990[6] and 1993[7], Joe Neisen writes about how important it is for LGBT persons, when in therapy, to explore feelings that have been hidden from others and to find the cost of denying and hiding these feelings and truths about self. He also emphasizes the need to look carefully and deeply at the attempts to "fit in" or "pass" and how that has reflected taking ownership of all the shaming messages that society dishes out. Neisen encourages LGBT persons to identify and wrestle with the anger that comes with these sacrifices. The important goal is to mobilize the anger and use it constructively to motivate change, rather than destructively directing it toward themselves. He equates the negative self-image that internalized homophobia represents and the resulting anger to a cultural victimization. For many, being gay was felt to be a personal defect and shifting the process to a healing mode is essential.

Regardless of how hard we work at it, those of us who have "different" families will always struggle with precisely what it means to be as comfortable as we portray on the outside. While my children will tell you the many gifts of coming from a "differently-daddied" family, I am sure they also can tell you many ways that it was not so easy and point to some major (at least at the time) conflict that arose out of it. I can also say that, when my daughter told me she wanted to be married at the Cathedral of Hope, whether or not I said it, my internal thought was "Why?" (I knew our families and knew this could create all sorts of questions and some challenges.) However, her answer was very clear: "This is my church home. It's a beautiful place, and I wouldn't want to get married anywhere else." Once again, the innocence of the child taught the adult a lesson: inclusion means inclusion, and belonging means everything!

The other lesson I have learned from my children is that the way to be accepted is to be accepting. Each one of them has handled the issues of our family differences in their own unique way. In fact, sometimes I think it has been harder for them to explain what I do as a psychiatrist than anything else about our family. They learned early on that my partner was going to be around and a part of the family. It quickly became a non-issue. On a flight to Disneyworld, a flight attendant asked my daughter if I was her father (the resemblance must have been positive), then asked, "Who's this?" in reference to my partner. My daughter simply exited the aisle casually, glancing over her shoulder and said, "He's with us." She dragged and pulled at us to get off the plane. She had more important things to move on to! My son, on the other hand, has had no difficulty being in the middle of it and showing off his "different" dad. By middle school, he loved to set up the conversation that always ended up with, "So what? Your dad doesn't look straight!"

I do think that they will tell you that one thing that helped them understand diversity was their experience on Sundays at the Cathedral of Hope. They got to go forward to communion, unlike the churches they attended with other family members. They were included in everything in the service. Even as they grew older, they continued to want to visit the Cathedral when they came home to visit. They could be introduced to couples of all sorts and to people who fit every stereotype and those who fit none. They could shake hands with someone in drag just as easily as someone who was intersexed. They often didn't even notice that people were different. I am convinced that being in such a large, diverse and inclusive environment taught them to be more open. They, in turn, taught me many new definitions of acceptance on a personal level.

Is there Good News?

The good news is that, once we face the grief and understand the impact of the loss, we can move on and find our way. We can never fill that gorge in our lives. Eventually, if we are lucky, we can begin to see how it adds to the geography and landscape of our hearts and lives, and gives us a unique beauty that can only come from the healing of grace. We learn to pause when we are faced with reminders and to revere the memory of the loss and how it moved us forward in life. In reality, the important thing is not the loss, but the growth that comes out of it. In a speech to the Society for the Advancement of Sexual Health several years ago, Wayne Muller described this process best when he said:

> *Somewhere, in the membrane between suffering and healing, there is a moment of grace, wherein something is broken down and something is broken OPEN.*

He reminded us of the smooth, round bulb that must face frost and then be ruptured in order to become a tulip or daffodil. That membrane is often very, very thin. We may not know it is even there in the pain, but we can count on the grace.

High Risk: Addiction, Cancer, AIDS and the Realities of Being Homosexual

I will not have done my duty as a psychiatrist and physician, if I don't talk a bit about "risk management." The fact is that being gay, lesbian, transsexual, intersexed or bisexual carries risks on many levels. My primary focus is mental and emotional health. However, we also must remember that the LGBT population also represents a disproportionate number of uninsured adults. We talk a lot about those at risk for HIV-related diseases, but LGBT people are also at risk for the typical human illnesses, and at higher risk for some illnesses, such as gynecological and breast cancers in non-childbearing women. Smoking-related illnesses are slightly higher than the average population, and other health risks related to lifestyle, eating habits and stress are also greater. In short, being in the middle of the bell curve, where anything in your life is pretty well accepted, makes for a healthier way of living with less work. Conversely, anyone who lives in secrecy or isolation or without ready support is at greater risk in general.

Addiction: It's not Just for Druggies!

Not only will I not have done my duty, but I surely will lose some laminated membership card if I don't talk about addiction. I have spoken about how drugs and alcohol are so much a part of the bar scene, the bathhouses and the overall perception of "the lifestyle." Yet, addiction is less about the chemicals than the relationship the person has with the way they make them feel and the illusion that "the world goes away." All too often the focus gets aimed at the "drug" as the whole problem. In reality, the issue is much deeper.

The issue in addiction is an intense drive to avoid what we in psychiatry call "negative affect." In lay language, bad feelings or emotional pain. I've already talked about how difficult it can be to grow up gay and in dysfunctional families. Sometimes it seems like a drink or a pill or something to smoke might just "lubricate" the situation and make life so much easier. This is compounded when our social circles are centered on drinking or "partying."

I also need to mention what we call the process addictions: gambling, food (anorexia, bulimia and overeating), sex, work, shopping, spending and so forth. These addictions are more subtle, more pervasive and more difficult to escape. Each of them has some presence in every person's daily life. Even someone who is celibate (or perhaps asexual) lives with a gender, a sexual identity and a sexual role each and every day. We all eat and take risks (a.k.a. gambling—think yellow traffic lights!). Like chemical addictions, the key thing about process addictions is that their sole purpose is to give the illusion that some form of discomfort—usually emotional or mental—doesn't bother us. Again, the "problem" is not in the bottle, the pill, the food, the sex act or the card game. It is in the relationship a person develops with the illusion of altered mood.

Problem? What's a Problem?

How do you know if you have a problem? Well, for the most part, if you asked that question, you may be on that road. Ask yourself a few questions and see how you answer:

- Do you tend to do a certain behavior as a reward when you feel good or when you feel bad?
- Do you set a limit on that behavior for yourself but, more often than not, exceed that limit?
- Do you try to stop that behavior because you don't like it or its effect on you, others or your life?
- Do you find yourself spending more and more time doing or preparing for that behavior, even though you would rather not do it?
- Do friends, family or coworkers ever complain about the effects of that behavior on your life?
- Do you sacrifice important people, activities or work because of this activity?
- Do you often feel guilty about that behavior?

If these questions bring some behavior into question, you may want to talk to a professional. Remember that the key is the relationship with the behavior and its ability to relieve emotional pain, not the kind, amount or frequency of the behavior. The pain doesn't go anywhere; it just appears to be gone for the singular moment that the addictive behavior creates.

One of the most powerful negative emotions that addictions attempt to cover is shame. Shame is the deeply rooted sense that not only is what we do bad, but we are inherently so defective at our core that we are worthless throughout. Many people mistake guilt (the sense that we have fallen short in what we have done) for shame. I believe that there is no such thing as healthy shame. I believe that what some people call healthy shame is embarrassment (the sense that the world has seen me for the fallible, frail, totally human person that I am). The major difference I see is that guilt almost always shows us a specific action to correct it. If I feel guilty for standing you up for dinner, I can reschedule, be there early and bring flowers! Shame, on the other hand, feels unchangeable, written in the stone of our soul. Nothing can change shame.

In his book *Out of the Shadows: Understanding Sexual Addiction*,[8] Patrick Carnes lists the four major core beliefs that are the foundation for addiction. While Carnes is speaking of sex addiction, I believe these can be modified to fit all addictions:

1. I am basically a bad, unworthy person.
2. No one would love me if they really knew me.
3. My needs are never going to be met if I have to depend on others.
4. Sex [or any mood-altering experience] is my most important need or sign of love.

These four statements succinctly describe the internal struggle that fuels addiction. Unfortunately, they also match, and seem relatively logical as, the assumptions that come from growing up gay or in a dysfunctional family. They are the messages of shame.

Because shame makes a statement about our basic makeup, being ashamed leaves us without any hope of ever changing or being different. As a parent, it was always difficult to give the message to my children that they were valuable, worthwhile and wonderful even when they made mistakes and did some pretty awful things. Who they are never changes! What they do is constantly developing and changing.

The primary antidote for shame is connection with others. I believe that only in the grace that comes from the genuine (sober), consistent, inclusive and accepting emotional embrace of others can we find the "data" we need to change the messages of shame. Therein stands the importance of community, whether it is in the church, the coffee shop or the living room.

Recovery? What's Recovery?

Rather than summarize the whole of addiction treatment here, I will make a few broad and sweeping statements:

- The goal of recovery is to reprogram the faulty core beliefs to:
    1. I am a worthwhile person, deserving of love and pride.
    2. I am loved and accepted by people who fully know me as I am.
    3. My needs can be met by others if I make them known and ask for them to be met.
    4. I have many expressions of my needs and abilities to care for others.
- Addiction is a system/family/couple's disease. It does not affect one person.
- Recovery doesn't happen alone.
- Recovery is a lifelong process for the addict and those closest to them.

That said, if you feel like some aspect of your life is out

of control, then seek out somebody whom you can trust and ask for help. If someone you love is out of control, walk with them. However, you MUST have your own healing process, too. Recovery involves changing not only the ways we think and act, but also our core belief system.

My usual analogy is that of Fred Astaire and Ginger Rogers. He got all the credit while she did everything he did, but backwards and in pumps! Well, when we are in a relationship (whether it is friendship, love or a family relationship) with someone who is in the throes of addiction, we often try to "backwards lead" them off the dance floor. Notice: you're still dancing! If they stop the addiction and we keep dancing, they either have to stand on the edge of the dance floor and yell at us, leave us or start dancing again. We have to leave the dance floor, get rid of the pumps and learn how to live differently, too. It doesn't work to send them to a therapist, a treatment center or a meeting to "get fixed" while we continue in the same dance or don't change our thoughts, beliefs or actions.

Healthy Homosexual Relationship: Isn't That An Oxymoron?

There is a story of a lost and brokenhearted gay man walking on a beach who finds a tattered, smashed and tarnished lump of metal. As he brushes off the sand, a bent, wrinkled, gruff old genie blunders out in a puff of grey smoke, grumbling, "Alright already, I was sleeping. You get one wish and make it quick!"

Adonis, as the gay man was known, thinks for a moment, drying the tears of the last broken heart. He thinks of the great escape. "I want a six lane freeway from here to Honolulu!" he exclaims with hopeful glee.

The genie chokes, stumbles back and launches into a

monologue about how impossible it is to do something like that. "Why the engineering feat that would be ... You've got to be out of your ... Forget it! Try again."

Despondent and in despair, Adonis goes for the next best thing. "I want a healthy relationship," he says.

The genie becomes very, very still, knits his brow, scratches his head and, after a deep sigh, utters in resolve, "How many lanes did you want on that road?"

I think this sums up how many people—whether LGBT, straight or something else—feel about relationships in general. Humans are so very complex that combining them is a challenge for the best of us. When the starting point for a relationship is the struggle of growing up gay with no clear or healthy role models and an umbrella of shame and guilt, the challenge gets even more complicated. Rev. Piazza has written about relationships already. I'll add my list of important qualities of a healthy intimate relationship:

- **Mutuality**: MerriamWebster.com defines mutuality as, "Having the quality of being mutual (or having the same or shared feelings for one another)." A healthy relationship involves finding and sharing common interests, understanding, values and emphasis in life. It involves all parties contributing support, guidance, constructive criticism and energy to the relationship.
- **Reciprocity**: Defined as, "The quality or state of being shared, felt, or shown by both sides" and "a mutual exchange of privileges," reciprocity is perhaps one of the more important qualities of a healthy relationship. Each person has a turn to be both the foreground and the backdrop of the relationship in varying degrees and over time. It is more than just taking turns; reciprocity means understanding the value of taking the back seat to what is important and valued in the relationship.

- **Consistency:** I like what MerriamWebster.com has to say about this one: "Harmony of conduct or practice with profession." Simply put, the relationship has a pattern of behavior that matches what we "profess" or say about the relationship. Maybe, this is the intent of the marriage vow that describes "for better, for worse, for richer, for poorer, in sickness and in health."

- **Honesty**: This is both easy and complicated. On one hand, it means we tell the truth to each other, simply and openly. On the other, it means we respond with kindness and openness. My rule of thumb is that, when asked a "yes or no" question, the answer is one of those two choices. Honesty, does NOT mean I tell you every sex act I did with my last partner to make you feel better. (However, I am not sure what the honest answer is to "Does this make me look fat?") Honesty DOES mean I tell you my feelings as clearly as I can and as promptly as I identify them, especially when they regard the relationship.

- **Joy**: To me, joy is the sense that, even when I am distressed about the relationship, I can reflect on something wonderful and it will always be true. I distinguish between happiness and joy this way: My son loves to take me for rides on roller coasters. When we are on the ride, screaming and poking fun at each other, we are happy. However, each and every time I tell the stories of our theme park adventures and roller coaster rides, I experience the joy over and over and over.

If I was teaching "Relationships: 101," this would pretty well sum up my syllabus! Volumes have been written, and much good direction is available out there. I suggest trying on some relationship skills either from people who have the kind of relationship you want or from a book that feels on target for both of you. In the end, what works is what works for you.

Healthy Sex: Now THAT'S an Oxymoron

Many of us grew up with the typical American message that sex is very dirty and we must save ourselves for someone we really love. We've talked about how homosexual (or otherwise "different") sex is often discovered and explored in the dark, clandestine areas of life. Most heterosexual adults can pretend to have no unusual curiosity and no "strange" thoughts.

However, let me offer an example of this falsehood. My office, which is across the street from a major medical center in Dallas and within shouting distance of two of the more affluent areas of town, is surrounded by sex and alcohol. None of the main streets to my office go more than two blocks without a minimum of one—usually two or three—liquor stores. Of the four directions one can go at the intersection in front of the building, one need only drive from two blocks to two miles to run into either a store with the word "condom" somewhere in its name, a boutique for "erotic" clothes and apparatus, or an adult bookstore. All of them not only have been present, but thriving for the entire seven years I've been in that office. I also might add that none of them are for the LGBT market and all of them market and window dress for the heterosexual couple. If all sex is "normal" (called "vanilla" in some circles) then no market should exist for even one of these six or seven businesses in the entire Dallas-Fort Worth Metroplex, much less in this small area.

Just what IS Normal?

Many years ago, I was taught by a group of patients in the hospital that, "Normal is a setting on the washing machine." My definition of "normal" is usually "whatever you happen to be doing at the moment." While I'm not sure this is a good starting place for talking about sex, I think both definitions point to the reality that what people do sexually is widely varied and changes over any period of time.

Within the LGBT community, many definitions of normal exist, and they are all both right and wrong. They are blatantly wrong, in my opinion, if they make some other set of behaviors wrong, just because they are different. For years, the psychiatric mainstream defined everything between members of the same sex as pathological or sick. After much ado, this mostly has changed.

Sexologists, or sex therapists, work diligently to help people uncover what turns them on, or, as we say, their "arousal template." Much of their focus is on "normalizing" behavior and understanding feelings. In a gross over-simplification, they work with people to help them understand their own feelings about sex, to accept them and to figure out how to express them in a healthy manner.

Part of the problem within the LGBT population is that internalized homophobia rears its ugly head in the judgments people have about sex. The Center for HIV Educational Studies & Training at Hunter College in New York did studies of men who have sex with men. Much of their research can be summarized very simply: higher shame leads to higher risk. For instance, a behavior that tends to carry greater shame or confusion (such as anal sex) most frequently will be associated with higher risks of unsafe practices. A person who is less ashamed and more self assured will be far more comfortable insisting that a partner use a condom or dental dam, or insist on using on himself or herself. Furthermore, men who are HIV-positive are less likely to disclose their status than men who are negative. In fact, if a person initiated a conversation about HIV status, they were more likely to be negative.[9]

Labels, such as "sodomy," "top," "bottom," "dom," "sub" and others, serve not only to perpetuate, but also to deepen the shame about the behaviors, especially, if they are not clearly understood. In general, the history of pathologizing sex (viewing it as somehow abnormal) goes deeper into the LGBT population than in the straight population. Unfortunately, the guise of treating sex addiction has also complicated this process. Some sex addicts use the same-sex "line in the sand" as a way of both excusing and separating out their compulsive, driven behaviors from what they want others to know about them. Conversely, many gay or bisexual addicts have tried to force these feelings out of their mind by labeling them "addictive" and are trying to "recover."

Early in my career, I'm not happy to say, I imposed this model on some of the men who came into my addiction medicine practice (before I trained in psychiatry). Through my years at the Pride Institute in Dallas, I learned that, not only was this ineffective, it was not the least bit useful. Plain and simple, it was misguided, even though I was following the guidance of "knowledgeable" people. (It follows me like all those years when we told parents that their newborns had to sleep on their stomachs and we know now that is absolutely wrong.) To their credit, the people that crossed my path never seemed to buy this line of thinking and found their way in spite of it.

Without taking on the volumes that have been written about healthy sexuality, I would like to list just a few of the things that I feel make for a greater likelihood of a healthy sex life. The National Leather Association International has a statement that I've borrowed over the years that, I feel, models a foundational concept of healthy sex. They speak of "Safe, Sane and Consensual" expressions of sex. I would add to them the fourth essential component: Sober. Almost every study and every story I've heard about either blatantly unsuccessful sex or high-risk sex usually starts with "a couple of drinks" or a "little bit of partying."

Here is where I emphasize one of my favorite "bumper sticker" mottos: "If it's that important today, it'll be that important tomorrow." If this IS Mr. or Ms. Right, the banner bearing that title will still be hanging on the bedpost in the morning. Sober up first.

The opposite is also very true: If you require mood-altering chemicals to engage in a behavior, then it probably is not one you are comfortable with and you may want to avoid it. Learn to talk about it and be comfortable with it sober, and then try it. Building on the healthy relationship characteristics of honesty and consistency, being able to express sexual feelings with a reasonable bit of embarrassment, but with openness while stone-cold sober is fundamental to a healthy sex life!

Here are some other things I think are important to a healthy sex life:

- **Communication, communication, communication:** In my lectures to my patient groups, I repeatedly tell them my acid test: "If you can't talk about it at the breakfast table, you probably don't need to be doing it in the bedroom." Getting past the embarrassment about sex begins with being able to have an open, adult conversation about it.

  During my years of working with gay men of all ages, I regularly ask them about "safer sex," and each one will tell me that they know all about it. When I "remind" them about the kinds of lubricant not to use with various types of condoms and ask them which flavor they prefer for oral sex, and then, in a bit of sadistic pleasure, ask them to demonstrate how to safely remove a condom, I find out that they don't have a clue about safer sex other than "put on a condom."

- **Consent:** Not only asking permission before crossing a line of personal behavior, but also as the process progresses. We really don't have to complicate this. It can be as simple as accompanying an initial move or gesture with "Is this alright?" or asking before hand, "Would you mind if I ...?[10] Then, an occasional, "How's this?" or "You enjoying this?" will go a long way to maintain consent. NOTE: The absence of an answer means "No" until otherwise stated!

- **Context:** Part of healthy sex is the context: who, what, where, when and how, defined by everybody involved. Mutual understanding about context is a huge part of creating the safety and understanding that come with intimacy. Personal preferences about time of day, location, lighting, "costume" and such things play in to the pleasure for all involved.

- **Boundaries, legal and otherwise:** There are some absolutes in terms of respecting partners. In general, minors (especially children), the infirm of all ages, and the aged, who have difficulty with thinking and memory, are protected by the legal system for a reason. These are always dangerous boundaries to cross.

- **Trauma resolution:** An individual can never truly trust and be open with the active echoes of trauma in their psyche, whether these are feelings of disgust and avoidance or actual flashbacks (mental replays of trauma in thought, sensation and feeling). The most graphic example is when a person who has been raped tries to participate in submissive role play.

This always will have the potential of re-enacting the trauma, with a huge adrenalin response. While this may feel almost identical to arousal, it is a risky place to go until the trauma has been therapeutically addressed and resolved. This does NOT mean ignoring or pretending it never happened!

- **"Baggage drop-off"**: By this, I mean it is essential to leave our emotional baggage not only at the bedroom door, but, preferably, a block or so away. This includes judgment about what is right and what is wrong. Fetishes are often assumed to be unhealthy and to be avoided. However, sexual arousal comes in a wide variety of shapes and forms and can involve any combination of all five senses. The essential element is choice. It is rarely healthy to be unable to perform sexually without external aids, any more than it is healthy to have only one or two means of expression of sexuality.

I probably could write for days and never cover all I want to here. Let me wrap up by saying that, as individuals, we are the only ones who know our own truths, including our sexual truths. The only way to find out what is really true for us is to be able to come out of hiding and talk, ask questions and express ourselves. This is most of all true in the arena of sex.

Being Homosexual is Difficult Enough, It Shouldn't Be Hard.

I'd like to close with words of encouragement and admonition: Be gentle. "Alternative lifestyle" is a grossly shame-based euphemism for saying something is wrong. To grow up in the confusion of the LGBT youth, and have so many things to dodge, overcome, avoid and escape sets up a tremendous struggle in and of itself. That struggle doesn't need to be complicated by shame, guilt, self-deprecation and sabotage. Furthermore, the rampant homophobia within the LGBT community always gets in the way.

If I've learned one thing in my years as a physician and as a psychiatrist, it is that I don't know all the answers; no one does. The "answers" are what we find along the way in our own individual journeys. Whether we're talking about our physical attraction, sexual behaviors or spiritual practices, each of us has a unique journey and perspective. If we don't learn to respect that, we end up becoming just another part of fads and turmoil within the community.

While this journey is extremely individual, we are "pack" or "herd" animals. We cannot, by and large, survive alone in the wilderness very well. We need the reflections, and the company, of others to help us understand ourselves. I thought I understood exactly what love was at the birth of each of my children. Each time, I fell madly and deeply in love with that newborn infant, mess and all. However, that understanding of love took a quantum leap when I watched as my grandchild, at two or three months old and from several feet away, lit up with a smile at the sound of my daughter, her mother's, voice. All it took was that sound and she not only felt safe, but was overjoyed and thrilled. To see that kind of love within the context of the love I have for my children, added multiple new dimensions to my understanding of how much we respond to and need others. It also reminded me that responding to others is a joyous thing.

Unfortunately, reaching out to others is fraught with perils. I regularly tell people that what human beings do best is "screw up" and make mistakes. If we give our hearts to others, they may (and probably will) hurt us in some big or small way. If we place our trust in other humans, we will, no doubt, eventually be disappointed. However, someone much wiser than me dared the one of us who is without mistake (sin) to cast the first stone.

Spending this lifetime around humans has brought me many times to that place where I wasn't sure if I was being broken down or broken open. Yet, it is the glimpses of joy, love, peace and sincerity that I get to see in the eyes of those around me and, especially, those whom I love that has found the way through those shattering experiences to grow a bit every time. That growth is what allows me to love as deeply and intensely as I do today ... mistakes and all.

1 The Diagnostic and Statistical Manual is the consolidated reference manual that is the academically agreed upon list of psychiatric diagnoses and conditions. It is entering its next iteration and is the result of a consensus of many of the "selected experts" in the field regarding what constitutes the criteria upon which a psychiatric diagnosis is based. However, the debate within the fields of psychiatry, psychology and counseling is never ending and is not absolute. Much like the Bible, the interpretations are legion and the precision is minimal. This is, in the end and in my opinion, a very subjective construct designed to help guide a very abstract and imprecise art and science to which many lives are entrusted.

2 A crude, colloquial reference to older gay men who "befriend" the lost young men who come into bars. It is not a kind term and one that might bear some looking at down the road as the gay community deals with its own internalized homophobia.

3 *Motivation and Personality* (New, York: Harper & Row, 1954).

4 Kubler-Ross, E (2005) *On Grief and Grieving: Finding the Meaning of Grief Through the Five Stages of Loss*, Simon & Schuster Ltd, ISBN 0743263448

5 O'Neil, C. and Ritter, K., Coming Out Within: Stages of Spiritual Awakening for Lesbians and Gay Men, HarperCollins, New York, NY, 1992.

6 Neisen, J., 1990. "Heterosexism: Redefining homophobia for the 1990s." *Journal of Gay and Lesbian Psychotherapy* 1(3):21-35.

7 Neisen, J., 1993. Healing from cultural victimization: Recovery from shame due to heterosexism. *Journal of Gay and Lesbian Psychotherapy* 2(1): 49-63.

8 Carnes, Patrick, PhD, *Out of the Shadows*, Hazelden, 1989. Center City, MN

9 Parsons, J.T., Schrimshaw, E.W., Bimbi, D.S., Wolitski, R.J., Gomez, C.A., & Halkitis, P.N. (2005). Consistent, inconsistent, and non-disclosure to casual sexual partners among HIV-seropositive gay and bisexual men. AIDS, 19 (S1), 87-98. Also, other articles from the same data.

10 Remember that consent CANNOT be given when an external power differential exists. Such things as an employer-employee relationship, gross financial dependence, the desperate need for "discretion" (a.k.a. secrecy), political or legal authority and other power components of relationships obliterate boundaries and make it impossible for the person with the least power to truly give consent. In addition, the survivor of sexual trauma, even if it is well hidden to the conscious mind, has great difficulty avoiding feeling like "damaged goods" and feeling deserving of being treated badly. This also eliminates the ability to identify choice and give full consent.

Resources

Amazing Grace, Malcolm Boyd and Nancy Wilson, eds. The Crossing Press, 1991.

Church and the Homosexual, The by John J. McNeill, Beacon Press, 1988.

Come Home by Chris Glaser, Harper & Row, 1990.

Coming Out Within: Stages of Awakening for Lesbians and Gay Men by Craig O'Neill and Kathleen Ritter, Harper San Francisco, 1992.

Don't Be Afraid Anymore by Rev. Troy Perry, St. Martins Press, 1990.

Embodiment: An Approach to Sexuality and Christian Theology by James B. Nelson, Augsburg Publishing House, 1978.

Embracing the Exile: Healing Journeys of Gay Christians by John E. Fortunato, Harper & Row, 1982.

Gay Priest by Malcolm Boyd, New York: St. Martins Press, 1986.

Gay Theology Without Apology by Gary David Comstock, The Pilgrim Press, 1993.

Is the Homosexual my Neighbor? Another Christian View by Virginia Ramey Mollenkott and Letha Scanzoni, Harper San Francisco, 1978.

Jonathan Loved David by Tom Horner, The Westminster Press, 1978.

Lord is my Shepherd and He Knows I'm Gay, The by Rev. Troy Perry, Nash Publishing, 1972.

Loving Someone Gay by Don Clark, Celestial Arts, 1987.

New Testament and Homosexuality, The by Robin Scroggs, Augsburg Fortress Press, 1983.

On Being Gay by Brian McNaught, St. Martin's Press, 1988.

Profiles in Gay and Lesbian Courage by Rev. Troy Perry and Thomas Swicegood, St. Martins Press, 1991.

Rescuing the Bible from Fundamentalism by Bishop John Shelby Spong, Harper San Francisco, 1991.

Social Tolerance, and Homosexuality: Gay People in Western Europe from the Beginning of the Christian Era to the Fourteenth Century by John Boswell, University of Chicago Press, 1980.

Stranger at the Gate by Mel White, Simon & Schuster, 1994.

Taking a Chance on God by John J. McNeill, Beacon Press, 1988.

Taking off the Masks by Malcolm Boyd, New Society Publishers, 1984.